IMAGES
of America

KEY LARGO

IMAGES
America

KEY LARGO

Brad Bertelli and Jerry Wilkinson

ARCADIA
PUBLISHING

Published by Arcadia Publishing
Charleston, South Carolina

Library of Congress Control Number: 2012940670

For all general information, please contact Arcadia Publishing:
Telephone 843-853-2070
Fax 843-853-0044
E-mail sales@arcadiapublishing.com
For customer service and orders:
Toll-Free 1-888-313-2665

Visit us on the Internet at www.arcadiapublishing.com

This book is dedicated to those who have lived these stories and shared them, as well as those interested in a glimpse into Key Largo's past.

CONTENTS

Acknowledgments 6

Introduction 7

1. Key Largo 9

2. Oversea Railway 19

3. North Key Largo 41

4. Planter 59

5. Tavernier 65

6. Planter Revisited 91

7. Rock Harbor 101

ACKNOWLEDGMENTS

This book would not have been possible without the support of the Historical Preservation Society of the Upper Keys and its two fearless leaders, Jerry and Mary Lou Wilkinson. Thank you to Tom Hambright, historian extraordinaire of the Key West Branch of the Monroe County Library as well as the families of the Upper Keys, who have been so generous over the years with not only their photographs but also their stories. Special thanks go to Everette Albury, Charles Lewis Pellicier, Ann Pellicier Dunn, and Loralea Carrera. As always, thank you to my family and my wife, Michelle. Your love and patience make my work possible. Thank you, too, fan No. 3. Unless otherwise noted, all images are from the collection of Jerry Wilkinson.

INTRODUCTION

The Spanish name for the island, Cayo Largo, roughly translates to "Long Island." Today, it is called Key Largo and though it is not the first of the Florida Keys, at over 27 miles long, it is the largest island in the chain. While today Key Largo is a playground for fishermen, boaters, scuba divers, snorkelers, and those looking for a sub-tropical escape, before running water, mosquito control, and air-conditioning were conveniences here, island life was not an easy one.

Once upon a time, Key Largo was a base of operations for Florida wreckers. They were not the rapscallions lore has painted them to be, but diligent sailors with a job to do. While wreckers patrolled the entire length of the Florida Reef in search of ships in peril, wrecking outfits tended to congregate where the action occurred, and the shallows surrounding Key Largo were a popular spot for one particularly good reason: Carysfort Reef. Located a handful of miles off the coast of North Key Largo, Carysfort has been statistically proven to be the single most dangerous tract of coral in the Florida Reef chain. In fact, the oldest recorded shipwreck in North America, the HMS *Winchester*, wrecked on Carysfort Reef in 1695.

Wrecking was not always full-time work, and most wreckers relied on other means to supplement their income. Some relied on the sea and worked as fishermen while others chose to farm. Rock melons, tomatoes, and key limes were fruitful crops. Ben Baker, considered the "King of the Florida Wreckers," supplemented his income farming pineapples on Key Largo.

Because of the importance of the Florida Straits as a shipping lane, the government began building the iron day markers and lighthouses that still dot the reef line today. As charts improved and ships switched from sails to the more reliable steam, shipwrecks along the reef became fewer and farther between. Like so many other industries that boomed and then went bust, the wrecking industry, too, failed.

Henry Flagler was the man who first linked the islands to mainland America when the Key West Extension of his Florida East Coast Railway crossed Jewfish Creek and rolled across Key Largo. While Key West was the final destination, Key Largo was the first point of entry and the last point of egress. Sadly, the train would prove to be a relatively short-term investment. The Key West Extension, however, was ultimately condemned after the Great Labor Day Hurricane of 1935, the most powerful hurricane ever documented in the United States.

While Flagler made Key Largo and the Florida Keys more accessible to mainland America, the train had not been the only way to reach the islands. By 1919, the Miami Motor Club was lobbying to create automobile access to the Upper Keys as a way of providing winter tourists a "suburban" fishing ground. Dade and Monroe County commissioners agreed to connect Key Largo to the mainland by constructing a road that would become known as the "fishing route." Today it is referred to as Card Sound Road.

It did not take long for tales of these fish-filled turquoise waters to spread. Fishing camps began to develop on the island, and the local fishermen began to find work as fishing guides to visiting tourists eager to create their own fish stories. To accommodate fishermen, new industries developed.

Visiting fishermen, including presidents, artists, and writers were lured to the islands and required hotels to sleep in and places to eat. Restaurants began serving succulent local fare like turtle steaks, cracked conch, and crayfish. While turtle steaks and fresh local conch can no longer be found on local menus, one constant has remained a year-round treat and that is key lime pie.

It is important to keep in mind that no two of these deliciously tart local desserts will taste exactly the same. It might be prudent to sample more than one of the tangy treats. Some visitors, in fact, go so far as to taste as many key lime pies as they can to determine for themselves who really does serve the best pie. There are practically as many signs advertising this claim as there are restaurants lining the Overseas Highway.

While these days the chamber of commerce refers to the island as the "Dive Capital of the World," Key Largo has always been a fishing community. The World Famous Caribbean Club, featured in the Humphrey Bogart and Lauren Bacall classic, *Key Largo*, started out as a fishing camp of sorts. Today, it is one of Key Largo's primary roadside attractions. The island is also home to John D. Pennekamp Coral Reef State Park, the world's first underwater park.

It is fortunate for everyone who picks up this book that Jerry Wilkinson is the historian responsible for gathering the images revealed in these pages. President of the Historical Preservation Society of the Upper Keys, he is a recognized expert on Key Largo. Wilkinson first came to the Keys in 1947 and remembers riding his motorcycle along the highway from Key West to Key Largo without passing more than a couple of vehicles traveling in either direction. While fishing from the bridges has been a tradition since the bridges were first built, it used to be that fishermen were able to spend the night camping right on them.

Life has changed on the islands over the years, and Wilkinson has spent decades trying to document everything he could. In the process, he has acquired a wealth of history about not only Key Largo, but all of the Florida Keys. Unless otherwise credited, the photographs and postcard images on these pages come from his collection.

The island of Key Largo has not been incorporated, but has been divided into three major communities including North Key Largo and Ocean Reef /Angler's Club, Tavernier (and formerly Planter), and the Rock Harbor area that is now referred to as Key Largo. What will hopefully become clear is that Key Largo is drenched in a boat-load of history and while this book is by no means a complete history of the island, it is a glimpse into one excellent story.

Welcome to Key Largo.

One

KEY LARGO

In the 1898 book *Our Country: East,* which is a compilation of works by different authors, Kirk Monroe writes, "The terrible Florida reef, with its bewildering maze of shoals, tortuous channels, fierce currents and coral heads lifted almost to the surface, is an ever present menace to the mariners of the waters. Since the date of its discovery it has probably been the cause of more disasters than any other region of similar extent in the world."

Corals, animals of the class anthozoa and related to jellyfish and sea anemones, build reefs. Individually, corals are called polyps and begin life as free-floating plankton. Maturation occurs when the polyp descends and settles on a suitable substrate. The polyp secretes limestone, which it uses like mortar to build a house. Remarkably, another polyp settles down and builds next door until a colony is eventually formed. Coral colonies create tremendous feats of architecture. Slow builders, it can take a decade for coral to build a structure the size of a coconut. The Florida Reef is the result of hundreds and thousands of years of slow coral growth. The above photograph is a close-up of a coral polyp. The photograph at left shows a collection of reef-building coral colonies. (Courtesy of the Florida Keys National Marine Sanctuary.)

The Florida Keys were once a thriving coral reef. Approximately 100,000 years ago, during the last North American ice age, the ocean receded and exposed the limestone substrate of a dead barrier reef system. The fossilized remains would become the Florida Keys. When Juan Ponce de León sailed past the coast of La Florida on his expedition to discover the Fountain of Youth in 1513, he named this archipelago Las Martyrs. What the intrepid explorer saw reminded him of sun-bleached bones, and he reportedly thought the islands had a tortured appearance. The Keys are not, generally speaking, lined with extravagant beaches. One of the reasons these Atlantic waters can be crystal clear is because of the relative lack of sediment clouding the water. There is not a great deal of sand in the water and certainly not enough to wash up on shore and cover the rocky substrate with a beach. This photograph shows a typical Keys shoreline relatively devoid of sand.

The Florida Reef is the third largest barrier reef system in the world. The two larger reef systems grow off the coasts of Australia and Belize. The Florida Reef is 358 miles long and stretches from the St. Lucie Inlet to the Dry Tortugas, 70 miles southwest of Key West. This is a photograph of Carysfort Lighthouse, found a few miles off the coast of North Key Largo. The light marks Carysfort Reef. The HMS *Winchester*, the oldest recorded shipwreck in North America, struck this reef in 1695. More shipwrecks have been attributed to Carysfort Reef than any other reef in this barrier reef system. The lighthouse was constructed in 1852. Lt. George Meade of the US Topographical Engineers oversaw its construction. Meade was eventually promoted to general; during the Civil War, he was one of the men responsible for leading the Army of the Potomac to defeat Robert E. Lee at Gettysburg.

One of the earliest recorded mentions of the island was a 1639 nautical chart noting the plot of land as the "Caio dos 12 ligues." In 1687, a different name for the island was recorded on a Spanish document after officials interrogating an English pirate, Ralph Wilkinson, reported reference to the island as Cayo Largo. The first time that name was written on a chart was by Spanish salvagers sent to recover treasures wrecked when the Spanish fleet was destroyed by a 1733 hurricane. One of the first times the words Key Largo were written on a map was the 1774 Bernard Romans chart. Key Largo is not the first island in Florida's most famous archipelago. It is, however, the largest island in the chain. Key Largo was once home to wreckers and farmers. Today, it is a haven for fishermen, scuba divers, and those relaxed souls toasting the sunset with a margarita.

Florida wreckers sailed along the reef line in search of ships in peril, sometimes in tumultuous weather. The first licensed wrecking captain to arrive on the scene of a shipwreck was deemed wreck master. The wreck master decided how a salvage operation would unfold and how many crews would be needed. He received the largest cut of the salvage award. J.B. Holder made this drawing of a salvage operation in 1860.

This J.B. Holder drawing of a Florida wrecker was made when he toured the Keys in 1860. Wreckers were required to save the crew, cargo, and, when possible, the ship. By 1860, they had to be licensed by the US government. Wreckers were awarded a salvage claim for their efforts, generally 25 percent of the value of all contents salvaged.

In 1852, Capt. Ben Baker was living in Key West. He was 32 years old. Captain Baker is historically referred to as the "King of the Wreckers." While he made his name out on the reef, Captain Baker homesteaded 160 acres on Key Largo, near what would be mile marker 97 today. Captain Baker, in fact, is considered to be the first to farm pineapples on the island, an industry that would, in its heyday, supply America with 85 percent of its pineapples. He became one of the largest producers of pineapples in the Upper Keys. While standing amidst his pineapple sprouts, he could scan the reef line with his spyglass for ships in peril. Captain Baker would also successfully petition to open Post Office Cayo Largo in 1870. Baker stated in his postal application that he planned mail distribution to 17 families.

A PINE-APPLE CLEARING ON KEY LARGO.

Another of Holder's sketches, this image is considered to be one of Captain Baker's pineapple patches. The accompanying text reads, "Mr. Baker, the owner who resides in Key West, is reported to have realized seven thousand dollars this summer from his crop of pineapples." The account, titled "Along the Florida Reef," appeared in an 1871 edition of *Harper's New Monthly Magazine*. Holder first explored the Keys in 1860 and 1861.

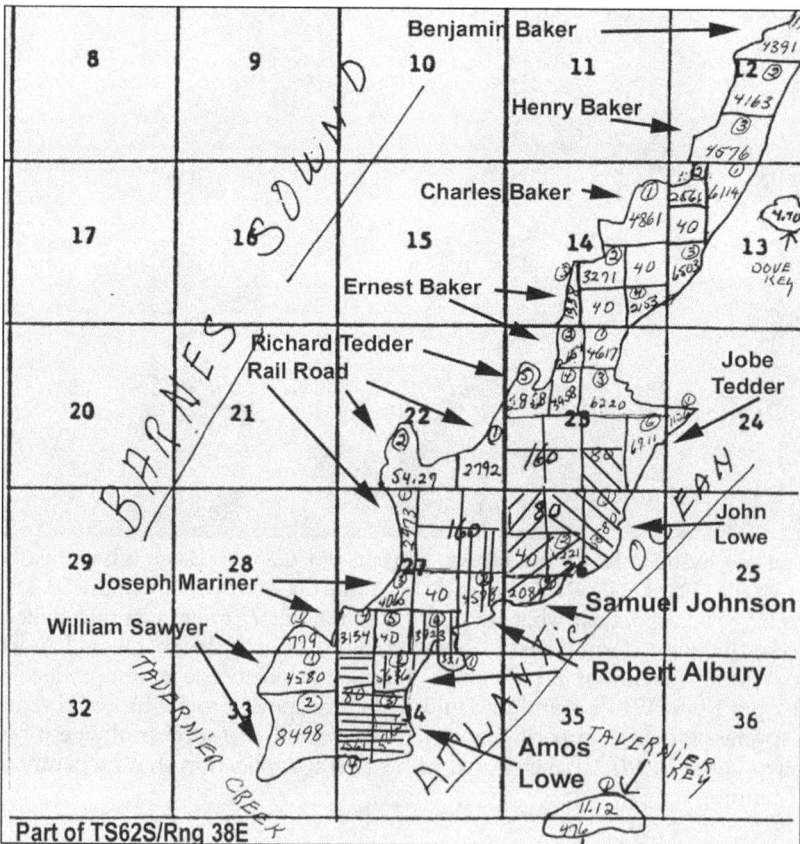

Part of TS62S/Rng 38E

Marcellus Williams conducted the first government survey of Key Largo in 1872. This map is from sheet No. 9 of that survey. He concluded, among other facts, that the island encompassed 23,622 acres. Drawn on the map are the approximate locations of the homesteads that had been approved by 1890. The names and general locations of the early families have also been included on the map.

16

The shipwrecking industry was all but over by the turn of the 20th century. The licensing bureau closed its doors in 1912. Another primary industry to energize growth in the Keys was farming. Early crops included pineapples, key limes, tomatoes, and rock melons, but like the wreckers before them, farming proved an unsustainable industry. The industry responsible for commercially developing Key Largo into what it is today is fishing. Whether for commercial or sport purposes, it was the need to house and feed the fishermen who came to cast their lines into these fertile waters that led to the building of hotels and restaurants.

The railroad, too, made an impact on the island. Key Largo was the gateway to the Florida Keys and Henry Flagler's Florida East Coast Railway began service from Miami to Key Largo years before the train arrived in Key West. The passenger train rolled across Key Largo when the Jewfish Bridge was completed in 1907. This 1933 photograph shows the train crossing the original Jewfish Creek Bridge.

While Key Largo is still a fishing destination, scuba diving, a competitive industry, asserted itself in the 1960s. The island attracted national attention when John D. Pennekamp Coral Reef State Park, the world's first underwater park, opened to the public in 1963. Over the years, scuba diving and snorkeling have become synonymous with Key Largo. The Key Largo Chamber of Commerce claims the island is the "Dive Capital of the World."

Two

OVERSEA RAILWAY

By 1907, the Key West Extension of Henry Flagler's Florida East Coast (FEC) Railway had reached beyond Key Largo. This photograph, labeled March 1907, shows Flagler's personal car stopped atop the Tavernier Creek Bridge. It would be five years before Flagler's private railcar would reach Key West.

Henry Morrison Flagler was born January 2, 1830, in Hopewell, New York. Young Henry moved to Ohio and worked as a store clerk for Dan Harkness. Flagler then moved to Bellevue, Ohio, to work for Lamon Harkness. Flagler married Lamon's second daughter, Mary. The image shows Mary accompanied by her sister, Julia. Henry Flagler would make his fortune in oil and would help bring the Standard Oil Company to fruition with Henry Rockefeller.

After making his fortune in oil, Flagler used his money to become a railroad-hotel magnate. At a meeting held by the Jacksonville, St. Augustine & Indian River Railway Company board of directors on April 19, 1893, Flagler declared, "The line of the company be changed so as to run and extend from some point on Biscayne Bay, in Dade County, to the Island and City of Key West."

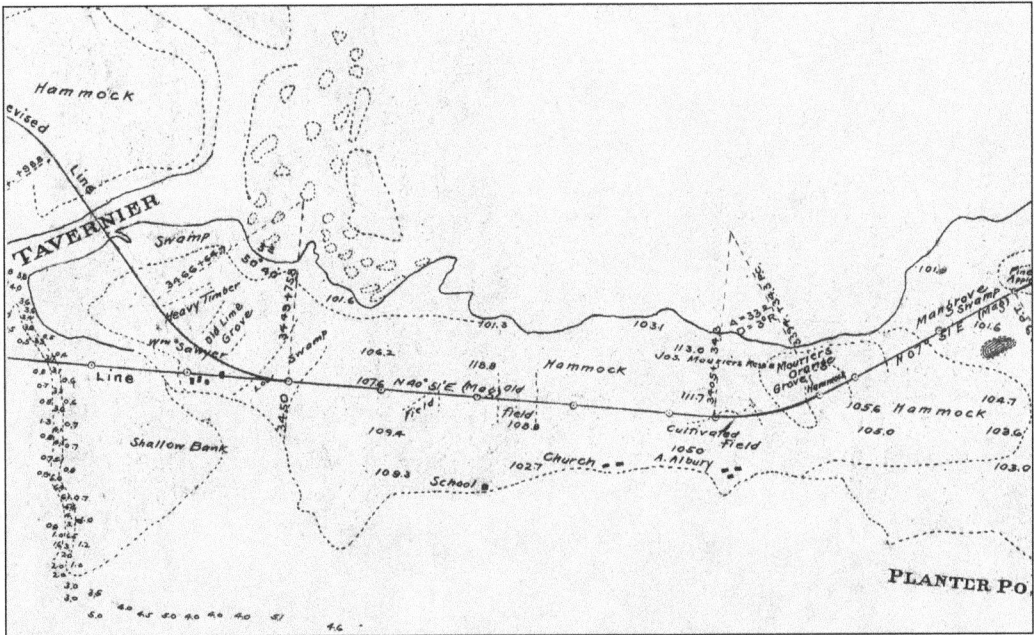

Engineer William J. Krome was hired on October 3, 1902, by Flagler's Florida East Coast Railway to determine the best way to connect the mainland to Key West. The surveys were completed by 1905. It was decided the route would cross Key Largo. This chart shows Krome's survey of the southern tip of the island. Krome submitted estimates regarding materials and labor costs with his surveys.

This photograph of the Key Largo survey crew was taken in November 1905. These men were responsible for mapping out the centerline of the Key West Extension of the railroad as well as pinpointing boundaries and establishing depths, heights, and the desired slopes of the track. Computations of these numbers made it possible to calculate costs associated with building the railroad, including the costs of pumping, loading barges, and handling water.

Construction on the Key West Extension of Henry Flagler's Florida East Coast Railway began in 1905. This photograph, taken that same year, shows one of the early Key Largo work camps. Work on the railroad appeared at several sites along the surveyed right-of-way simultaneously in Key West as well as Key Largo. Each work camp consisted of a mess hall, officers' tent, medical tent, commissary, and barracks. The men pictured here represent the whole gamut of the railway operation, from those responsible for clearing the thick subtropical hardwood hammocks that once covered the islands to those tasked with surveying the subtle turns and grades of the route. The work was dangerous, backbreaking, and miserably hot, yet these men appear to be wearing long sleeves, and jackets in some cases, to help protect them from the clouds of mosquitoes that savaged them. Note, too, there are at least six dogs pictured in the front row.

This 1905 photograph was taken inside a work camp tent office. There is no qualifying evidence, but the paper stacks on the table to the left are thought to be charts. It is interesting to see that the men have their pants tucked inside their boots. Likely, at least in part, this is to combat the mosquitoes. Note that the boy leaning against the pole is barefoot.

In the spring of 1905, a fleet of dredging barges made the trip south from Miami and were sent to multiple worksites throughout the Keys. Four dredges were assigned to the 18-mile stretch area. Two barges dredged their way south from the mainland, and two dredged their way north from Jewfish Creek. This is the dredge *Mikado* at work in the creek on March 16, 1906.

C.B. Wilson wrote to W.J. Krome after coming upon a body of water he was not expecting to find. It was dubbed Lake Surprise. Wilson wrote, "The lake has but one out-let, a small creek leading out of the most easterly mouth of Jew Fish creek into Black-water Sound. This creek is narrow varying from 25' to 35' in width and from 6' to 10' deep. With a small amount of work the creek can be opened so that boats can enter the lake." By the time this photograph was taken in 1906, a causeway across the lake had been created by using fill. Fill was piled up until a stretch of earth was created. Enough debris was dumped along the path that eventually a support base developed. The men in this photograph are pitching ballast stone over the sides of a flatbed railcar.

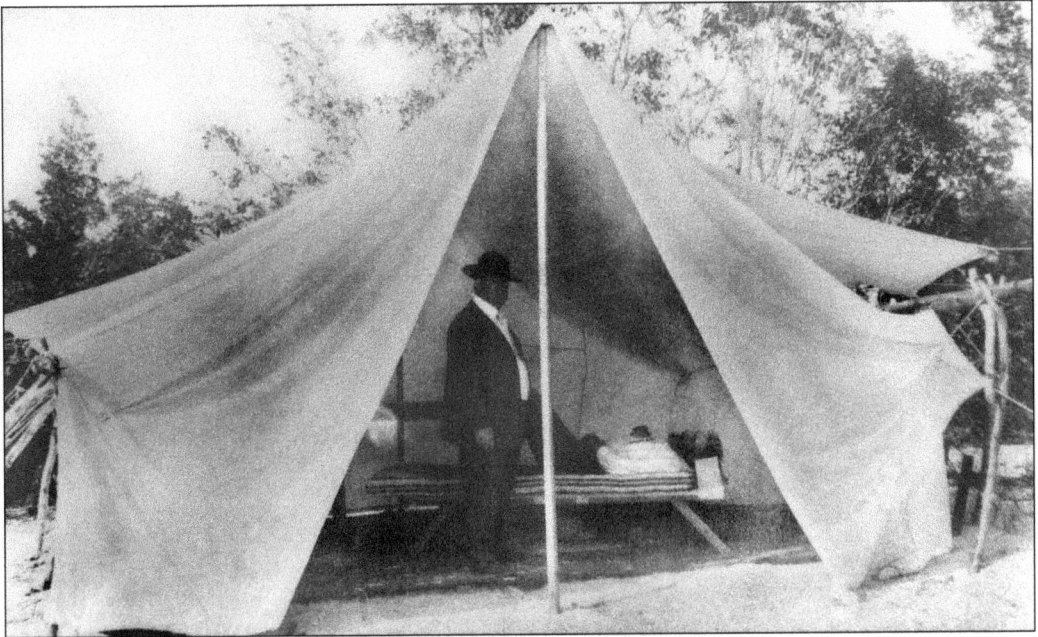

This photograph, taken April 12, 1906, shows one of the medical station tents provided at each of the FEC Railway work camps. Free medical services were provided to all railway workers. Railroad field medics tended to injured workers. For more serious cases, Henry Flagler maintained a well-equipped hospital in Miami that was overseen by Dr. James Jackson. Dr. Jackson became the namesake of Miami's Jackson Memorial Hospital.

The 124-foot steam powered stern paddle-wheeler Wanderer was brought from the Mississippi River for use as a ferry and transport for the railroad. In October 1906, a seam in the hull sprung a leak while tied up to a dock. About 30 minutes later, six feet of water covered the main deck. The ship was raised and towed to Miami for repair.

A Krome diary entry reads as follows: "This body of water which we call Lake Surprise is nearly two miles long by 1 mi wide and from 6' to 8' deep with rock bottom. It is entered from both Blackwater Sound and Barnes Sound by obscure hidden creeks and is not shown on any map or chart. We had no idea of its existence and it has played awash with all my calculations." The view appears to be looking south toward Key Largo. An early version of the causeway appears to have been completed. While not technically a bridge, the undated photograph seems to be from November 1906 and represents one of the first water passages of the Key West Extension. Lake Surprise would not be the last body of water to test the resources of the men responsible for completing Flagler's Key West Extension.

The last completely dated photograph of the Lake Surprise project was taken November 29, 1906. It appears to be sufficiently filled, and the causeway completed. The barge dropping off its load for work to the south carries mounds of railroad ties. Telephone poles have been placed along what is now the 18-mile stretch between Jewfish Creek and Florida City. The Jewfish Creek Bridge would open to traffic in two months.

The southern railway tracks veer to the right, traverse a makeshift bridge, and connect to the barge carrying the No. 10 locomotive engine arriving from Lake Surprise on November 23, 1906. The engine rolled on to the tracks directly from the barge. The tracks were rediverted and connected to the line stretching south from the mainland. The No. 10 was a valuable addition to the labor force.

On December 17, 1906, Henry Flagler and his staff visit Key Largo to inspect the progress of the Key West Extension of his FEC Railway. Of the eight men standing atop the railcar, Flagler is the fifth man from the left. He is sporting a top hat and his signature bushy moustache. The 76-year-old Flagler surveys the work being done in his name.

Manatee Creek was initially an entry point for dredges to create fill from the east side of what is now the 18-mile stretch. Survey teams knew there was fresh water in the Everglades, but they did not know where it was. After the dredges arrived in Manatee Creek, survey teams discovered the vast quantity of fresh water it could provide.

Construction of the railroad required about five million gallons of fresh water every month. It was fortunate that Manatee Creek, found near what is mile marker 112 today, proved an excellent source. Railroad workers built a pumping station at the creek. The fresh water from the creek was pumped up through each of these pipes and emptied into cypress holding tanks, which were then transported by the train.

Cypress water-holding tanks were placed atop flatbed railcars. When the train stopped at Manatee Creek, the pumps were opened up and a series of tanks could be filled simultaneously. The creek proved to be one of three fresh water sources used by railroad workers. The other sources were found in the Homestead area to the north and on Big Pine Key to the south.

By November 1906, construction at the Jewfish Creek Bridge site was well underway. In this photograph, a work barge is in the foreground while a steam-driven pile driver is on the left. In the background, a line of fill on which the tracks will be placed can be seen. The focus of this image is the men working to complete the bridge's center cofferdam.

This is the view from inside a cofferdam. Friestiedt steel sheet piling had been forced into the substrate by a steam-driven pile driver. The photograph, taken June 4, 1907, shows what a cofferdam looked like once the walls had been set in place, the bottom had been sealed, and most of the water pumped out. The image is from a real-photo postcard taken by a Florida East Coast Railway photographer.

Coffer means "box," and a cofferdam is a box dam that is created in order to produce a dry environment for work that will be done below water level. During construction of the Jewfish Creek Bridge, cofferdams were created by using metal interlocking sheets driven into the substrate using a steam-driven pile driver. Once the structure has been created, a concrete sealant was poured around the edges, the water was pumped out, and the cofferdam was filled with cement. In this photograph, the bridge's two end cofferdams are shown. They stand equidistant from the center cofferdam. This image looks west toward the mainland. Note the cofferdams intersect the raised railway bed pictured in the background. The boiler pipe visible in the left corner belongs to a work barge anchored in Jewfish Creek.

Pile driver

Draw Bridge

Concrete
Abuttment

Bull
Gear

This photograph shows the nearly completed Jewfish Creek Bridge. In the background is the pile driver barge with a cypress fresh water tank behind it. The end cofferdams have been replaced by concrete abutments, and the center cofferdam has been fitted with a bull gear mechanism. The bull gear is attached to the Jewfish Creek Bridge and allows the bridge to swing open to allow boat traffic to pass through.

When this photograph was taken April 7, 1907, the 100-foot swing bridge was in the process of rotating open. The wooden structure on the right is possibly for the bridge tender. There appears to be a small loading dock next to the building, suggesting that both boats and trains were unloaded here.

The men grasping poles in this June 1906 photograph are drilling. Their steel rods are equipped with star-drill points, and their job was to drill holes into the limestone substrate big enough to insert a stick of dynamite. Once a series of adequate holes was formed, dynamite crews stepped in and set their charges. It was dangerous work, responsible for an estimated 21 deaths and a host of lost appendages.

Once the dust from the blasted dynamite settled, a crew was sent in to harvest the bits and pieces that had been blown free. Where space provided, mule-drawn carts were backed up and loaded with debris. In the image, some of the drillers seem to be taking a break while others appear to be back at work.

Dynamite blasting was used to clear land. The debris field left behind was picked up, loaded, and carried away. The photograph seems to be an overview of the operation. The men standing to the left are drillers. The tracks of the Oversea Railway are clearly established at upper right. The men filled the side-dump car with debris, and then the mule was prodded until it began pulling the car along the track. The operator decided where to dump the load. With the push of a lever, the load could be dumped to the right or the left. Once the bed of the right-of-way was firmly established, all the narrow-gauge tracks were dismantled. This photograph is thought to have been taken at approximately mile marker 105.

This photograph depicts how the narrow-gauge tracks were used to create the bed of the railway across the Dove Creek slough. Dove Creek was located at what is now mile marker 93. Because it was a depressed area, it required fill to create level railroad tracks, so a temporary bridge was created over the area. A side-dump car was filled with marl and rolled across the bridge, where its load was dumped until a base was created.

On May 28, 1907, the *Key West Citizen* reported: "When the F.E.C. Railway was first completed to Homestead and later to Jewfish Creek, an occasional passenger train was sent down to accommodate sightseers. Later, it was found necessary to inaugurate a daily passenger train to accommodate the hundreds of settlers arriving in the district." Multiple worksites had been engaged. This June 1906 photograph shows tracks on Upper Matecumbe Key.

Church services were provided to all Flagler railroad workers and conducted at designated areas at each work camp. Planking served as pews. The services provided were nondenominational. The above photograph was taken April 13, 1906. According to a caption associated with the image, "A workman is preaching. Reverend Father Kennedy seated in foreground."

It was 10:43 a.m. on January 22, 1912, when the train safely delivered 82-year-old Henry Flagler to Key West in his private railcar. Mayor J.N. Fogarty welcomed him. In a short speech delivered by Flagler, he said, "Now I can die happy. My dream is fulfilled." Three days of celebration ensued. The 100-year anniversary of the train's arrival in Key West was celebrated in 2012.

Flagler would die May 20, 1913, at the age of 83. The death was attributed to injuries suffered from a fall down a grand staircase. He died at his ocean cottage, named "Nautilus," in Palm Beach. Three days later, his body was shipped to St. Augustine, where it was laid to rest beside the body of his first wife, Mary Harkness.

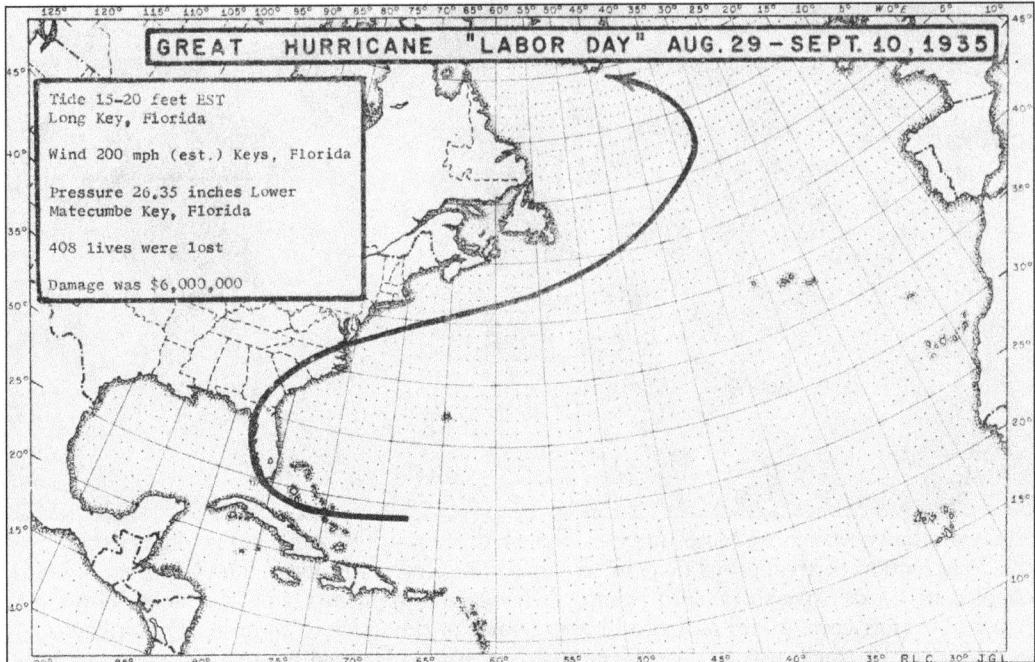

GREAT HURRICANE "LABOR DAY" AUG. 29 – SEPT. 10, 1935

Tide 15-20 feet EST
Long Key, Florida

Wind 200 mph (est.) Keys, Florida

Pressure 26.35 inches Lower
Matecumbe Key, Florida

408 lives were lost

Damage was $6,000,000

A hurricane formed in the Atlantic Ocean on August 29, 1935, and began to churn toward the Florida Keys. The Category 5 storm crossed Lower Matecumbe Key on September 2, Labor Day, with wind speeds approximated at 200 miles per hour. Across parts of the Upper Keys, the storm surge exceeded 17 feet. Called the Great Labor Day Hurricane, barometer readings plummeted to 26.35 inches, the lowest ever recorded in the United States.

This train had been sent to Matecumbe to retrieve the crews of World War I veterans working on the construction of an automobile counterpart to the Oversea Railway. The Category 5 winds, coupled with extensive storm surge, toppled the train and pushed it off its tracks. The Great Labor Day Hurricane would prove to be the demise of the Oversea Railway. The only car left standing on the tracks was locomotive engine No. 447. This aerial photograph taken after the storm shows a blank white area where the Islamorada Depot once stood. The debris field would have been found just north of Islamorada's hurricane monument, the Florida Keys Memorial, at mile marker 81, which commemorates the tragedy.

The Labor Day storm proved the end of the Key West Extension of the Florida East Coast Railway. In lieu of repairing the railroad tracks, the railway was disassembled. Some of the wooden cross ties were used as rail guards, and some were used to build storage structures and houses. Work converting the railroad right-of-way into the Oversea Highway began in 1936. This photograph, taken in 1937, shows a bridge being converted to accommodate automobile traffic.

The Great Labor Day Hurricane of 1935 destroyed Flagler's railroad. However, with the help of ferry service, automobiles had been able to drive along State Road 4A from Miami to Key West since 1928. This photograph shows a chain-driven dump truck working on Key Largo around 1926. The truck belonged to the Jenner Construction Company, the company under contract to build the road.

A headline from Homestead's *Leader-Enterprise*, dated November 10, 1939, declared: "Abandoned Roadbed of F.E.C. To Provide Short Cut to Keys-New Highway Is Sought By State." The land occupying the right-of-way from Florida City to Key West was purchased after the 1935 hurricane for $640,000. The purchase eventually deleted 14 miles from the road to Key West. The new passage bypassed Card Sound and State Road 4A, deleting seven miles of the drive between Florida City and, roughly, mile marker 106. One of the additions to the project was the construction of a new bridge at Jewfish Creek. The cost of the proposed double-leaf bascule drawbridge was $150,000. An April 7, 1944, *Leader-Enterprise* headline read: "Shortened Oversea Road Will Be Opened May 13." The year inscribed into the concrete of this undated photograph of the Jewfish Creek Bridge indicates that it may have unofficially opened earlier.

Three

North Key Largo

The first desire for a highway connecting Key Largo to the mainland was delivered in a political address given by George W. Allen in 1895. The Miami Motor Club lobbied for a road to the Upper Keys in order to provide winter tourists with a "suburban" fishing ground. In 1922, officials from both Dade and Monroe Counties allocated funds toward construction of State Road 4A. This 1926 photograph shows a dredge creating fill.

Dade County commissioners agreed to finance 11 miles of roadway between Florida City and Little Card Point. In 1926, Monroe County floated a $2.5 million bond for road improvements including a drawbridge to connect Little Card Point and North Key Largo. This team of workers, photographed in 1926, is likely associated with the Jenner Construction Company. The vehicle is spraying an asphalt-based sealant onto State Road 4.

This wooden bridge, called a swing bridge, traversed Card Sound and connected Key Largo to the mainland. Before it was completely constructed, the bridge was damaged by a 1926 hurricane. When repairs were completed, the bridge was elevated several feet. When the passage was opened in 1928, a hand crank was used to swing the bridge open. Later, a gasoline engine was used.

42

KEY INN.
KEY LARGO, FLA.

Because fishermen were able to drive from the mainland to Key Largo along State Road 4, Fern and Ed Butters opened the Key Inn in 1926. It was located about five miles south of what is today the Card Sound Bridge. Their restaurant became one of the first eating establishments along the road to Key Largo. They sold the property in 1928, moved south to Upper Matecumbe Key, and purchased the Russell Arms Hotel.

MABEL'S PLACE :: Key Largo, Florida
Famous for Lime Pies and Conk Chowder

Mabel Harris bought the Key Inn in 1928 and renamed it Mabel's Place. The highway sign at right advertises "shore dinners," and while the skeleton key on the sign likely references the Butters's Key Inn, it might also indicate the opening of other doors. Mabel's Place was famous for more than key lime pie and "conk" chowder.

MABEL'S PLACE — Kitchen
Craw Fish and Turtle Steak
Key Largo, Florida

Back in the kitchen, Mabel's chef was hard at work cooking up some of the local delicacies. Turtle steaks were popular fare in the 1920s. Crawfish, or the Florida spiny lobster, still is. The chef is holding up a tray of lobster. Because of the rapid decline of turtle populations, turtle became a protected species, and their steaks disappeared from local menus decades ago.

MABEL'S PLACE
Shore Dinners
Key Largo, Florida

Mabel's Place was alleged to have been not only a brothel but also a tearoom. In the Prohibition years, "tearoom" was a common code name for an establishment that served alcohol. Historically, however, what Mabel might best be remembered for is being the sister of Harry Harris, who would become a prominent local politician.

44

Where North Key Largo ends, a myriad of creeks, islands, and islets begin. This aerial photograph shows Linderman Key. The white line at center is a bridge, road, and dock linking Linderman Key to the Atlantic Ocean. The island is named after Bert and Jean Linderman. They were Canadian botanists who settled down and built a house on this remote outpost. When they moved to the island in the 1930s, they built a mansion and named the property Pirate's Lair. After Bert died, Jean donated the house to the University of Miami. The house was subsequently leased to the CIA, where it was used as a safe house. Linderman Key was also used as a training ground for the failed Bay of Pigs assault. In addition, scenes from an episode of the 1980s television show *Miami Vice* were filmed here.

Thord Ivor Hallström was born in 1878. A Swede by birth, he became a warrior by choice. As a mercenary, he participated in 13 wars including a stint in the Mexican Revolution as a member of Pancho Villa's artillery division. He changed his name to Ivor Thord-Gray in 1899 and moved to the United States in 1925, where he bought land on North Key Largo and built a house called Grayvik House. The Grayvik property is now part of Ocean Reef.

Jack Graham, who fished Key Largo waters in the early 1900s, enticed a group of North Dakota land buyers to purchase North Key Largo property. W.A. Scott, of Fargo, acquired the property and built a two-story coral rock house in 1912. In 1932, property rights transferred to the Roney Investment Company, operators of Coral Gables's Biltmore Hotel and Miami Beach's Roney Plaza. This 1933 photograph shows an early image of the exclusive fishing club.

In 1933, when this picture was taken, guests of the Florida Year-Round Club were delivered from Miami in the height of style and luxury. The car is pulling a luxury trailer where fishermen venturing to the exclusive club were able to relax in the relative comfort of a fine, though portable, resort room. VIPs were transported to the club via the Auto-Gyro, pictured here flying in the background.

The Auto-Gyro was not quite an airplane and not quite a helicopter. First developed by Spanish-born Juan de la Cierva in 1920, thrust was derived from a forward propeller, and lift was established by free-spinning "helicopter" blades. The Auto-Gyro was capable of safe, low-speed flight. To be transported from Miami to Key Largo by Auto-Gyro was swanky business indeed.

KEY LARGO ANGLERS CLUB.
THE FISHERMAN'S PARADISE, KEY LARGO, FLORIDA.

The Florida Year-Round Club became the Key Largo Angler's Club, a subsidiary of Henry L. Doherty's Cities Services Corporation. The club was first managed by Dave Curtis. What this postcard, postmarked April 4, 1941, shows is at least part of the two-story coral rock house, first built by W.A. Scott in 1912. The house was expanded to accommodate the club's main dining room.

In 1946, the property was sold to CAMRAY Corporation, formed by former Florida Year-Round Club manager Clint Campbell and Nina and Don Rayburn, a wealthy Michigan petroleum producer. Campbell and his wife became the resident managers, and with renewed interest and new investors, the club went through a renaissance of sorts. One of the new improvements was the construction of the breakwater and dock shown in this 1950 postcard.

48

Herbert Hoover was born in Iowa in 1874. The son of a Quaker blacksmith, Hoover was raised in Oregon. In 1891, he attended Stanford University, the year it opened, and graduated with a degree in mining engineering. Hoover became the 31st president of the United States, serving from 1929 to 1933. What might not be as well known was that he was an avid fisherman, who quoted from a 2,000-year-old Assyrian tablet: "The Gods do not subtract from the allotted span of men's lives the hours spent on fishing." Because of his strict Quaker upbringing, the president always dressed in a full suit, including jacket, white shirt, and tie, even while fishing. He is pictured here displaying the day's catch at the dock of the Angler's Club. Originally, 100 people were granted membership. Pres. Herbert Hoover was one of the first.

The Angler's Club was not President Hoover's original Florida Keys fishing destination. When he first started venturing down to the Keys, he spent time at the Long Key Fishing Club, first established by Henry Flagler and made internationally famous by author Zane Grey. Though Westerns were Grey's forte, that man loved to fish too. In any case, Hoover spent time at the Long Key Club, Craig's Camp, and Bill Thompson's dock in the Marathon area before he relocated to North Key Largo and became a member of the Angler's Club. Pictured in this photograph are President Hoover and one of his early fishing guides, Slim Pinder. Pinder is holding the fishing rod. The man standing on the other side of the president is identified as Don Bowers. The young man sitting down is unidentified, but the man sitting beside him is Hoover's longtime friend Larry Richie.

The fish that President Hoover wanted to catch was a sailfish. He finally accomplished the feat while in Miami to write the inaugural speech for his presidency. Hoover went out aboard the *Amitie*, a yacht loaned to him by Joseph H. Adams. This photograph shows the president standing with a sailfish. Larry Richie is holding the fish's tail.

This painting hangs above the fireplace at the Angler's Club lounge. The president is depicted with another of his favorite fishing guides, Calvin Albury. They met after Hoover admired Albury's casting technique, as well as two large bonefish he landed. The following day, the president sought Captain Albury's services. Albury, too, was curious about a man who fished while dressed in a full suit.

What the initials superimposed on this image of Grayvik Harbor mean remains undetermined. What the photograph reveals is a glimpse into the early development of the Ocean Reef property. Gen. Ivor Thord-Gray once owned 80 acres of land incorporated into the Ocean Reef property. Grayvik Harbor is one of two acknowledgments to the general. The other is Grayvik Drive. Morris and Alice Baker incorporated the land when they bought 40 North Key Largo acres in 1946. Morris was a real estate developer from Minnesota and originally wanted to purchase the Angler's Club. It was not for sale. His brother Alan, who had been living in Homestead, told Morris about the Despatch Creek Fishing Camp, and Morris bought the 40-acre property without seeing the site. By the end of the 1950s, the "fishing club" would incorporate 1,300 acres and grow to officially become the Ocean Reef Club in 1969.

This postcard was postmarked February 12, 1949, three years after prominent architect George Coffin designed the Ocean Reef Inn. Channels were dredged, docks built, land filled, and roads were created. Bathrooms at the inn were serviced by a water tower. Because of the difficulties in 1950 water transportation, bathroom signs at the property once read: "Don't take a shower 'til you smell; We haul our water and it costs like hell."

After Morris's death in 1959, the property was run by his sons William and Roger, who operated Seabound Properties, Inc., a subsidiary of Baker Properties, Inc. Property improvements were made, including construction of villas, golf courses, and country clubs. In October 1959, the price of a house designed by Coral Gables architect Edward Rempe, according to an article in the *Miami Herald*, was $25,000. William Baker stands to the right.

On March 3, 1969, the Baker family sold their interest in Ocean Reef. It would prove the most expensive single property transaction in the history of Monroe County. Harper Sibley Jr., a financier and Ocean Reef property owner, along with Miami developer Morris Burke, purchased Ocean Reef for $8 million. After Sibley and Burke purchased the once intimate fishing club, the name officially changed to the Ocean Reef Club.

Ocean Reef became accessible by land, sea, and air when the property's private airstrip opened in 1956. Dedication ceremonies for the 2,000-foot landing strip were held May 18–20. By 1980, the 15-minute flight from Miami International Airport to the Ocean Reef Airport, aboard Ocean Reef Airways, cost $28 one way. The airline went back and forth to Miami 20 times a day.

Florida's crude oil discovery program passed the Florida Oil Discovery Award in 1941. The bill commissioned a $50,000 prize to the first company to discover crude oil in Florida. Humble Oil won when it struck oil near Immokolee in the Everglades. This wildcat derrick, erected in the late 1940s, was built off County Road 905 in North Key Largo. The road passing behind it leads to what was called Dynamite Docks. The narrow channel entering the Port of Miami prohibited the safe delivery of dynamite, so the explosive loads were shipped to a long pier south of Ocean Reef extending into the Atlantic. The dynamite was used to clear land as well as canals. The dock became known as Dynamite Docks and was a hot-point for smugglers and drug trafficking.

A nuclear missile site became operational on North Key Largo in June 1965. It had two parts, an HM-40 Nike Hercules missile site and a missile guidance site. The radar system was located about one mile south of the Card Sound three-way stop. The missiles were located about another 1.5 miles south along State Road 905. Pictured is the dimpled, geodesic fiberglass radar-dome. The guidance system had a 150-mile range. It closed in June 1979.

This c. 1959 postcard depicts fishing camps along State Road 4A, once the lone automobile conduit bridging Key Largo and mainland Florida. Built in the 1920s, the road made the turquoise waters accessible to Miami fishermen. In the 1960s, around 100 people lived in the Card Sound area. Thirty were registered Monroe County voters. A handful of "restaurants" survived here, including Fred's Place, Bob and Lou's, and Alabama Jack's.

There was also Smitty's Fish Camp. This 1938 picture shows Earl Howard "Smitty" Smith with his two sons, Earl Jr. and Bert, inside the dining room. The camp could once be found between the present-day tollbooth and the bridge. The legacy of Smitty's fish camp was carried on through his sons, for a while, until it was washed away first by Hurricane Donna in 1960 and then Hurricane Betsy in 1965.

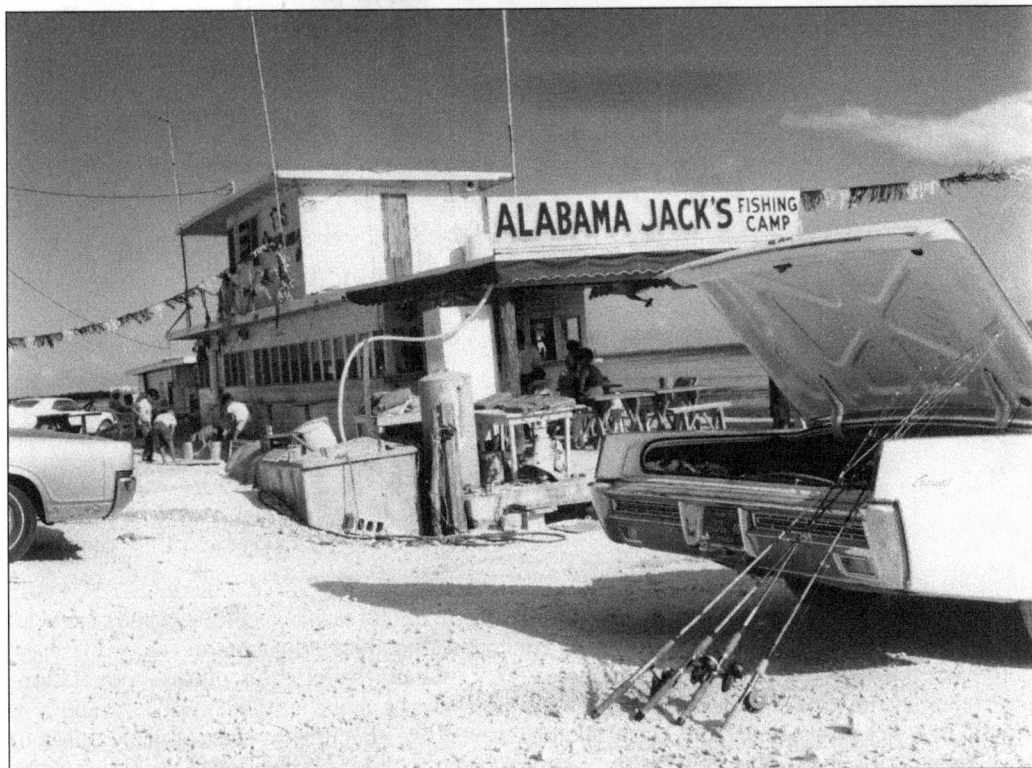

Jack Stratham lived in New York City, where he worked as a riveter during construction of the Empire State Building. Because of his Southern accent, Stratham supposed, he was given the nickname Alabama Jack. Later, Stratham moved to the Card Sound area and leased the property now called Alabama Jack's from a Miami plumber in 1953. Stratham's wife, Alice, loved to cook and was famous for her crab cakes.

The Everglades are a unique ecosystem and the only place in the world where alligators and crocodiles coexist. These are not saltwater crocodiles but American crocodiles. Alligators and crocodiles have both been considered endangered species. Because of their protected status, alligator populations have made a whopping comeback. Not too long ago, it was thought that there were only hundreds of wild American crocodiles left in the area. However, like the alligator, crocodile populations have begun to rebound thanks in part to Key Largo's Crocodile Lake National Wildlife Refuge, established in 1980. The refuge, found in North Key Largo, is comprised of 6,700 acres of tropical hardwood hammock, mangrove forests, and salt marsh. While American crocodiles are still fairly established in the tropics, the only place in North America where they can still be found is South Florida in general and Key Largo in particular. Due to successful management of the American crocodile, they have begun to re-establish themselves throughout the Upper Keys.

Four

PLANTER

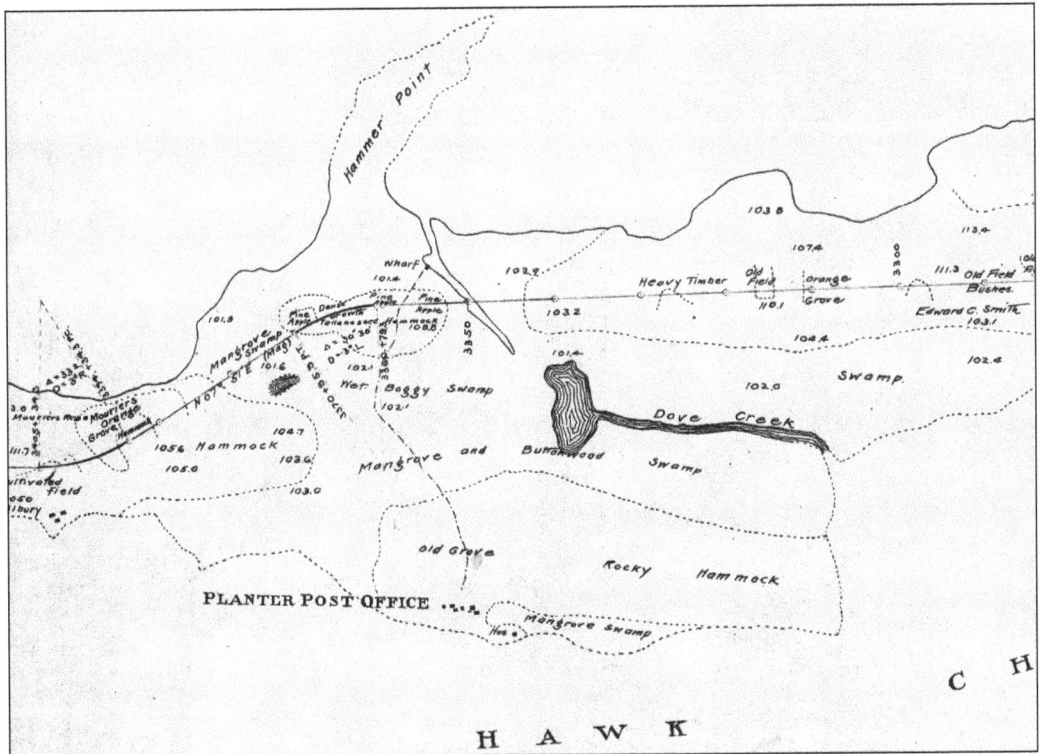

South Key Largo attracted some of the island's earliest settlers. The first to arrive were the Lowes, who homesteaded in 1880, and the Alburys, who homesteaded in 1882. The Johnson family, however, helped to define the community of Planter. The name Planter stems from how the community first made its living, by planting pineapples. The map, one of Krome's survey maps, shows the railroad right-of-way traversing South Key Largo.

Samuel S. Johnson was born in Great Harbor, Bahamas, but left the island when he was 18 and sailed to Key West. In the late 1870s, Johnson moved north to South Key Largo and became a homesteader. He met Caroline Tedder, and the two married. They had seven children and their brood would grow to become one of the founding families of Planter.

This is an early photograph of the Planter Pier. Before the railroad carved its way across Key Largo, boats were the only way to reach the islands. This pier used to be about the only way goods were trafficked in and out of the Planter community. These uneven boards, built to traverse the seagrass and limestone substrate, reached out into the Atlantic like an artery.

There is a loading dock at the end of the long pier stretching out from the shore of the Planter community. It was not the only pier, as another had been extended from the shore closer to the buildings to the left. Before the railroad, these docks were the lifelines of the community. Most of the buildings in this photograph, taken about 1900, are Johnson homes and businesses.

John Wesley Johnson established the Planter Post Office on December 31, 1891. At the time, it was the only post office in operation in the Florida Keys outside of Key West. He also operated a grocery store in a small building next to the post office. John Wesley lived in the house to the left of the post office. His father, Samuel Johnson, lived in the house to the right.

Religious services in the Upper Keys were first provided by "circuit riders," men of the cloth who traveled to isolated communities. By 1881, two Methodist ministers, Somelian and Giddens, were servicing the Upper Keys. The Florida Methodist Conference appointed Rev. J.M. Sweat to the Key Largo circuit in 1887. The first permanent Upper Keys church was established in Planter, on November 25, 1887. This picture is not of the church, but it does show the Planter parsonage, the house where the men of worship would stay, in the middle. The other two structures belonged to members of the Johnson family, with the house in the foreground at left belonging to Simon Johnson and the structure in the background at right, with the large porches, belonging to John W. Johnson.

This postcard image was taken on November 15, 1907, and shows members of the Planter community gathering in front of the church. The bottom of the postcard reads: "Sunday just before church. The message on the side reads: Dear Ida, Could not get No 3 Douglas shoes. Had No 2 but did'nt [sic] know if they would suit. No stove polish I send the sapolio, Love to all – Vivian."

Tom Johnson was the second of five boys born to Samuel and Caroline Johnson. In 1909, he was living in this house. The photograph seems to indicate the house survived a hurricane that struck the area. Debris litters the front. The 1909 hurricane was the third storm to strike in five years; another hurricane would affect Planter in October 1910.

The oceanfront community of Planter collapsed for two primary reasons, a pineapple blight and a series of hurricanes. Additionally, the Keys were no longer an isolated collection of islands accessible solely by boat. By 1910, railroad service had been established up and down Key Largo, and families had begun to relocate away from the coastline. The Planter Post Office closed in October 1910, and as the oceanfront population of Planter dwindled, families moved closer to the railroad tracks. Edward Payson Johnson, the youngest of the Johnson brood, can be seen above sitting on the steps of his Planter home beside his wife, Charity. They had three children, Edward, Jinnie Mae, and Ralph, the youngest. At right is an undated portrait of Ralph holding his two children. Edward and Charity were the last Johnsons to leave oceanfront Planter.

Five

TAVERNIER

This 1965 photograph shows Clara and Doug's Grocery, featuring beer, wine, and Western Meats. The picture also shows Tavernier Key, the small island in the background. Prior to 1775, the island was called Cayo Tabano on most Spanish charts. Roughly translated, the name means Horsefly Key. Eventually, Cayo Tabano was corrupted into Tavernier Key. In the early 19th century, it was a popular anchorage for wreckers.

The Tavernier Post Office opened March 9, 1911. The first postmaster, Daniel W. Riley, resigned the position 22 days later. The office then closed and reopened January 21, 1916. Merlin, the son of William and Ada Albury, Key Largo homesteaders, took over the post and served as postmaster for 10 years. The original post office building no longer exists. Merlin Albury and Jeanette Tedder, pictured here, married in Key West.

The Monroe County School Board minutes of September 8, 1914, indicate John Roberts requested an improved school for Planter. This one-room wooden building was probably the original Tavernier school. A school had to have 10 pupils. Students as young as four were admitted in order to reach 10. Teachers came from Key West and stayed with a host family. The teacher in this undated photograph is Elise Warren.

This image is of Robert Harold Albury's two-story house, located at approximately mile marker 92, Oceanside. The Albury family lived upstairs. Downstairs, Tavernier's second post office was in operation. Albury became the postmaster on July 31, 1926. The post office closed its doors at this location in 1961 and moved across the street. Today, the post office is located in Tavernier Towne shopping center.

Oliver M. Woods moved to Tavernier in the late 1920s. He was an early developer of the community. As well as real estate holdings, Woods was a builder and businessman. One of his first business ventures was the Standard Oil station pictured in this photograph, taken around 1927. Woods would take on partner Hugh Mackenzie, a teacher from Dade County.

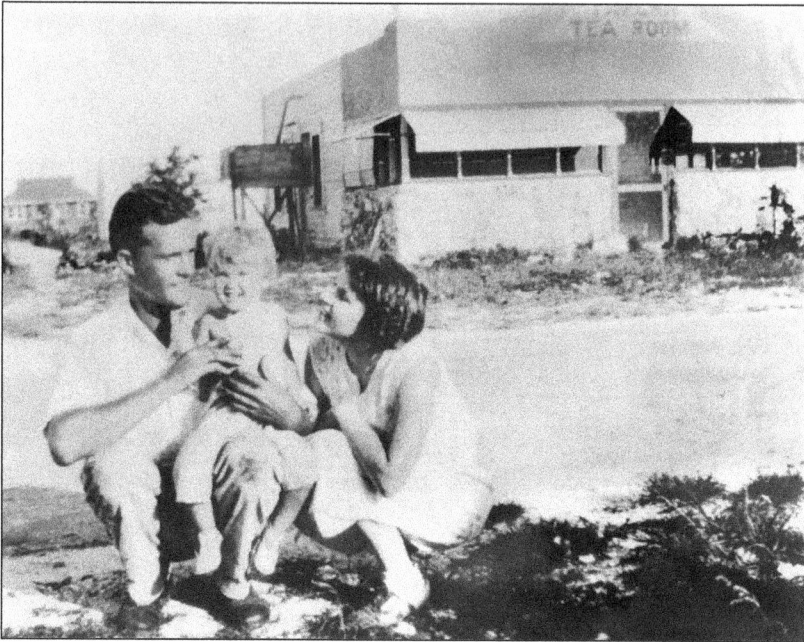

H.S. Mackenzie moved to Tavernier in 1928 with his wife, Hazel, and their baby, Joanne. Hugh was his given name, but everyone called him Mac. One of Mac's first jobs was operating the Tavernier Tearoom, a drinking establishment. Gambling was also rumored to have occurred on the premises. The empty lot next door would become home to the Tavernier Hotel.

The Tavern Store sold sundries, cold sodas, and ice cream. It was another of Mac's businesses, like the icehouse across the road from the gas station. Mac's architectural influence is still a strong presence in the community. The Tavern Store building is still there, next door to the Tavernier Hotel. For years, it was the Copper Kettle restaurant. In 2012, it is Café Moka. The Better Food Store appears under construction next door.

Mac was involved with Wood's Standard Oil station, too. This photograph, taken about 1932, shows Mac's first Standard Oil delivery truck. Ralph Gillespie is the deliveryman. Another of Mac's drivers was Harry Harris. Harris operated a truck fitted with iceboxes to accommodate home delivery of ice, another of Mac's services. Ice was nearly as precious a commodity in those days as oil.

Here are the students of Tavernier School in 1934. They are, from left to right, (first row) Lee Donaldson, Everett Albury, Madeline Albury, and Joanne McKenzie; (second row) William Ray Albury, Edward Albury, and Anthony Albury; (third row) Elizabeth Albury and Avis Albury; (fourth row) Charles Albury, Marjorie Albury, Jenny Seymour (teacher), and Mary Elizabeth Albury.

O.M. Woods moved to Dade County, which is where he died in 1934. Where Woods left off, Mac moved forward. This c. 1933 photograph depicts the business center of a burgeoning Tavernier community. Looking at the buildings, from left to right, the first is the Better Food Store. The next is the Keys Theater, Mac's second movie venue. His first motion picture enterprise was an outdoor theater; he showed films to locals as well as some of the 750 World War I veterans who were sent to replace the ferry system currently in place with automobile passage across the Keys. During the construction years, off-hour entertainment options were few and far between, and Mac's theater was a popular distraction. The next building is the Standard Oil station. Mac's icehouse was on the other side of the road and out of view. The photograph was taken from the top of one of Mac's petroleum storage tanks. Note the water tower behind the theater.

It was 1929 when Bea and Mac arrived in Tavernier. While their last names escape historians, the two ladies were trained nurses who, on the advice of their doctor, packed up their Dodge sedan and moved south for their health. They made camp on the Key Largo/Oceanside quadrant where Tavernier Creek distinguishes Plantation Key from Key Largo. When they first arrived, Bea and Mac slept in their sedan. They removed the back seat of the Dodge and used the vehicle to haul rocks, enough to build up a spot near the creek so that it was high enough to keep the tide at bay. The ladies then built a house. At night they would catch shrimp in the creek; by day, the dwelling was operated as a bait house for fishermen. Apparently, it is possible to take the nurse out of the emergency room, but not the emergency room out of the nurse. Bea and Mac also tended to local injuries and, in the worst cases, packed the wounded into their Dodge and drove them to the mainland.

By 1935, Mac had decided to expand his movie theater operation. The completion of the concrete block structure was nearing when the Great Labor Day Hurricane struck. The most powerful hurricane ever recorded in North America killed more than 420 people. A great many were World War I veterans. Mac's unfinished building became a Red Cross center. The small sign hanging in the door reads "First Aid Station."

Hours after the 1935 hurricane blew across the Upper Keys on September 2, the American Red Cross was providing on-site assistance with a first aid station organized at the second incarnation of Mac's Tavernier Key Theater. Mrs. Bishop, a Federal Emergency Relief Administration relief director for the area, is seen discussing a rebuilding project with a worker at the Tavernier headquarters.

The Great Labor Day Hurricane was not only a Category 5 hurricane but also the most powerful storm ever recorded in the United States. It devastated the Upper Keys. The storm produced 200-mile-per-hour winds and a 17-foot tidal surge. Water literally washed over the Upper Keys. This photograph depicts damage to downtown Tavernier. The railroad depot was destroyed when a house, pushed off its foundation by the tidal surge, struck it. The lone foundation visible to the south of the highway used to be a key lime packing plant. Fresh fruit was sold along the highway, daily. Later, the building was used as a sort of overflow school as the Rock Harbor School had outgrown its location. The dark line running from left to right is the railroad track. The white line is the old highway that used to run more or less parallel to the railroad tracks.

With the Oversea Highway nearing completion, the hundreds of World War I veterans who had once milled about after work hours in search of something to do had moved on. Mac finished his movie theater, as this c. 1937 image shows. The economy was suffering and the theater would be short lived. The Tavernier Tearoom, located next door, became Harry's Place and was serving turtle steaks.

This photograph, taken from atop Mac's petroleum storage tanks, was shot on June 21, 1938. Tavernier had rebounded from the 1935 hurricane and was growing. Along the northbound lane, at right, are signs advertising RC Cola and Nehi "in your favorite flavor," along with Wagner Daily Double lager beer. Not seen are the hardware store and repair shop. Outside of Key West, this was the only one-stop shopping center in the Keys.

This photograph shows a close-up of Mac's Standard Oil station featuring Atlas Tires and Ford parts. The Tavernier Key Theater is out of frame to the right, and the Tavern Store is to the left of the gas station. Note the telephone poles have been fitted with electrical transformers. The first attempt to supply the Upper Keys with electricity was done by Mac in conjunction with Florida Power and Light. Mac installed a 50-horsepower diesel generator behind the Tavern Store. Electrical lines stretched south to Geiger's Packinghouse at the corner of the highway and Coconut Row and north to where the Driftwood Trailer Park stands today. Service was provided from 5:00 a.m. to 10:00 a.m. and 5:00 p.m. to 10:00 p.m. and until midnight on Saturdays. Pictured from left to right are Ralph Gillespie, Dick Bland, and Louis Pellicer.

On November 17, 1913, Mervin Sterling married Amutal Arias in Key West. He was a fisherman. The couple moved to Tavernier and, in 1929, lived in this house. They survived the Great Labor Day Hurricane of 1935. The photograph was taken in 1937. In 1966, the Sterlings were two of Tavernier's oldest residents. On June 28, 1966, the board of county commissioners voted to designate the unnamed street where they lived Sterling Drive.

This is Mac standing in front of his empire along the Tavernier stretch of the Oversea Highway. The boy is Mac's son John. Mac saw the changing economics, closed the movie theater, and began converting the building to accommodate a burgeoning tourism industry. Here, windows are being carved into the building and sealed. The Tavernier Hotel conversion was completed in 1939.

During World War II, there were more than fish in the Atlantic waters off the coast of the Florida Keys. German submarines prowled the waters. This photograph, taken in 1942, shows Tavernier resident Jesse Alley checking out a live submarine mine that had broken free from its mooring and washed ashore near Tavernier. These mines would detonate when a vessel came into contact with one of the detonators that stick out from the bomb like a toggle.

HARRY'S PLACE
72 Miles South of Miami
Tavernier, Fla.

Harry Harris decided to get into the hospitality business when he opened Harry's Place, also called the Tavernier Café, in the building that was once the Tavern Tearoom. This postcard was postmarked 1941. Harry's Place was the first drinking establishment outside of Key West to acquire a liquor license. Harris saw that booze was a commodity, and Tavernier lacked a licensed distributor.

77

Harry Harris helped his sister out at Mabel's Place in North Key Largo before moving south to Tavernier where he would drive the Standard Oil truck for Mac Mackenzie. Harry also delivered ice, an act that brought him inside people's homes. He met people and got to know them, which served him well when he decided to enter Monroe County politics. He ran for constable in 1940 and lost. Two years later, he was elected to the board of county commissioners. This photograph shows Harris (right), sitting next to Pres. Harry Truman. County Commissioner Joe Allen is at left. Harris represented the Keys for decades. In 1975, while the mayor of Monroe County, he was indicted for bribing two county commissioners in exchange for supporting land development projects. Florida governor Reubin Askew relieved Harris from his duties on April 22. The charges were later thrown out, and Askew reinstated Harris as mayor on October 16.

Capt. Roy Tracy and his wife, Frances, moved to Florida in 1916. Roy opened a marine repair facility on the Miami River. They came to the Keys to lounge and fish and eventually retired in Tavernier in 1937. In the foreground stands the Tracy house. Frances was a registered nurse at John Hopkins Hospital back in Maryland and volunteered her services during the Spanish-American War.

Frances Tracy became known as the Angel of the Keys because she administered her nursing skills to the local community until she was 85, tending to bruises and cuts and removing fishhooks. She also set broken bones. For serious cases, she packed the patient into her car and drove them to Homestead or Miami. Today, the Upper Keys Garden Club meets at the Frances Tracy Garden Center at mile marker 94.

The Florida Keys Electric Cooperative formed in 1940 and eventually provided reliable electrical service from the Dade-Monroe County line to the Seven-Mile Bridge. Bolstered by a petition signed by 300 residents, the Florida Keys Electrical Cooperative purchased the holdings of Florida Power and Light, as well as those of Mac Mackenzie, for $6,230. This is a photograph of the first public Fairbanks Morris electric generator operated in Tavernier.

One of the men who helped install the generators at the Tavernier facility was Roy Tracy. The plant came online December 1, 1942. The diesel-powered generator was located behind Mac Mackenzie's Tavern Store, and Austin Reese was the plant's first operator. Ultimately, demand overwhelmed the plant's ability to adequately supply service.

Doug Killingsworth was a trained fireman from Homestead before he moved to Tavernier. He and his wife, Clara, bought Tavernier's grocery store in 1945 and renamed it Doug's Grocery. Mac Mackenzie originally constructed the building. Eventually, a fire station was built on the north side of the building. This photograph, taken around 1947, shows the building in its last days.

The next incarnation of the grocery store was the concrete building under construction in this photograph. The original Doug's was torn down and became the parking lot for the new store, Clara and Doug's Grocery. The building can still be found at mile marker 91.8. For years, it was the Sunshine Market. It is now the Sunrise Market.

The house in this photograph was built in 1919 and used to belong to Leonard and Hannah Lowe. The Lowes deeded the house to George Geiger on October 26, 1931. It can be found at 105 Coconut Row. The photograph shows the house after a garage was built onto the original structure. The garage has since been torn down, and the building has been restored to its original form. When George Geiger owned the building, key lime groves and tomato plants stretched from the highway to the Atlantic Ocean. Geiger used the building for two purposes. While his family resided on the second floor, the downstairs operated as a packinghouse for the tomatoes and key limes that were harvested from the field and readied for shipping. It is said that George Geiger lost a leg due to complications arising from a rattlesnake bite.

President Roosevelt addressed the annihilation of wild cotton in the Upper Keys in 1933. More than 20 Works Progress Administration workers were assigned to Tavernier, and another 20 were assigned farther north on the island. As well as cotton, those workers eradicated snakes, concentrating on rattlesnakes. John Curry killed this Eastern Diamondback rattlesnake on Key Largo. Carl Sawyer is holding it.

Tavernier's Driftwood Lodge was open for business in 1935. The *Florida Keys Weekly News* reported on June 7, 1947, that "Mr. and Mrs. Ray Maloney are now operating the Driftwood Hotel for the summer season. The dining room is now open and seafoods and Key lime pie are being served. Mr. Adrian Rollini, the owner, will be down to meet the public on or about Nov. 1."

Adrian Rollini was born in New York City in 1903. He was reportedly a child prodigy, taking piano lessons by the age of two and giving 15-minute recitals at the Waldorf Astoria Hotel by the age of four. He would become an internationally renowned jazz musician, a contemporary of Benny Goodman. He was best known for the bass saxophone but could apparently play just about any instrument. One of his favorites was the xylophone. Rollini also loved to fish, which drew him to Tavernier where he opened his Driftwood Lodge near the Atlantic end of Sunrise Drive. The dog standing on the pier is alleged to have been a picky eater and would only eat when Dorothy or Adrian Rollini fed the dog fish by hand. The lodge fell into disrepair after Adrian's demise in a Homestead hospital on May 15, 1956. Hurricane Donna finished off what was left of the building in 1960.

During World War II, the Coast Guard used a building behind Harry's Bar to house offices, barracks, the mess hall, and communications. George Marshall built this observation tower so that citizen volunteers could become a part of the Ground Observer Corps. The structure once stood near mile marker 91, Oceanside. According to the sign, children under 15 were not allowed on the tower.

By the 1950s, Mac had built a small empire along the Tavernier stretch of the Oversea Highway. He constructed the new Standard Oil station seen here at left. This was also the site of the Greyhound bus station. During World War II, seven or eight buses loaded with Navy personnel might stop for a comfort break. At far right is the hardware store, featuring Hotpoint appliances.

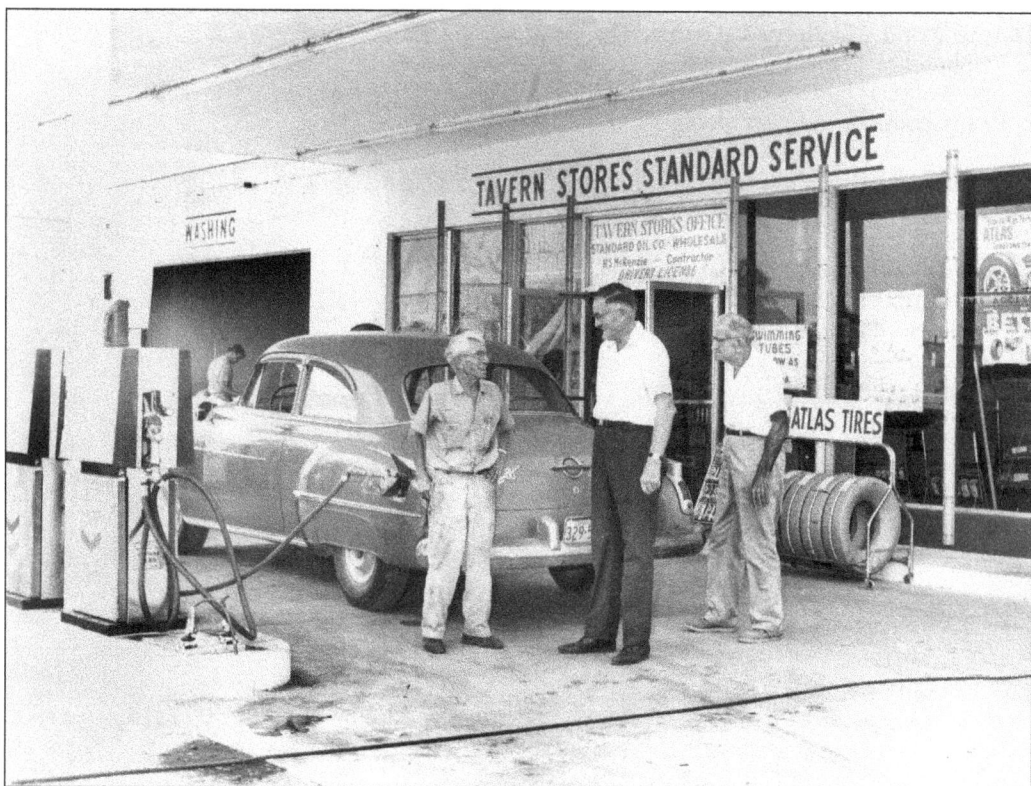

This is a close-up of Mac's new Standard Oil station, located across the Oversea Highway from the original. The Tavern Stores Standard Service still features Atlas Tires. Swimming tubes are also for sale. Mac is the tall man in the center. Note the car washing bay to the left.

Alonzo Cothron helped Mac construct Tavernier. Among other buildings, he was the contractor responsible for the movie theater, now the Tavernier Hotel. His business partner was Berlin Felton; today, their name still adorns one of Key West's better restaurants, the A and B Lobster House, overlooking historic Schooner Wharf.

This building has a twin, the Islamorada Library on Upper Matecumbe Key. Both were built in response to the Great Labor Day Hurricane of 1935 and both served as schools and hurricane shelters. In December 1951, the Tavernier building opened as the nonprofit Florida Key Clinic, Inc. The Florida Keys Clinic Board, spearheaded by Harry Harris and Frances Tracy, lured Dr. Harvey Cohn and welcomed him as the Upper Keys' first full-time doctor. Cohn was the house surgeon at Victoria Hospital in Miami. His wife, Dorothy, was a registered nurse. Fortunately, he liked to come to the Keys to fish. Dr. Cohn left his Miami practice on March 26, 1953, and came to Key Largo for what had first been agreed upon as a three-month period. It did not, apparently, take long to convince the good doctor and his wife to retire here permanently.

"Deadly Donna" holds the record for remaining a fully formed hurricane for the longest length of time in the history of Atlantic hurricanes. The storm attained hurricane status on September 1, 1960, and was a hurricane until sometime between 8:00 p.m. September 12 and 2:00 a.m. September 13. This is a photograph of the Tavernier Creek Bridge after Hurricane Donna blew over the Florida Keys as a category 4 storm. The image is looking east across the bridge and shows not only the washout but also the repair crew at work. While the bridge itself survived with minimal damage, the causeways leading up to it suffered washouts. Because of the creek's currents, scrap cars were dropped into the washout area to help create a secure base for the new fill. Barely visible on the right side of the causeway is a dump truck emptying fill. Also visible, just barely west of the bridge rail, is the freshwater pipeline from the mainland.

This building used to be the Tavernier Methodist Church. The original church building was located in Planter and was destroyed by the 1935 hurricane. It was rebuilt in 1936 from scavenged debris from the storm and later moved to this locale on Tavernier Street where, in 1959, it became Masonic Lodge No. 336. The Monroe County property appraiser took this photograph in 1965.

This 1965 photograph shows an Alpine Sunbeam parked in front of the office building of county commissioner Harry Harris. He is sharing space with Herbert Love III, a bookkeeper. The building was once home to Harry's Place, site of the first liquor license issued in the Keys outside of Key West. Next door, the hotel is advertising efficiency apartments. Harry's Place moved across the road to a bigger building.

Harry's Place moved to a bigger building across the street. In addition to featuring all the Keys traditions like turtle steaks and key lime pie, the restaurant also operated as a package store for those looking to purchase a bottle of liquor to take home. This postcard of Harry's Place is from about 1946.

The new concrete Masonic Lodge, at right, was built in 1981. The community formed the Old Tavernier Town Association and purchased the old wooden structure and some lots along US 1 where the building is being moved. The Sunday school annex was removed when it was relocated to its present location at mile marker 91.7. The building now houses the offices of the *Free Press* newspaper.

Six

PLANTER REVISITED

Robert Thompson founded Key West's Thompson Cigar Company in 1915. The company moved to Tampa in 1920 and remains the oldest mail-order cigar company in the United States. It holds Tampa's Postal Permit No. 1. Thompson's daughter Hilda remained in Key West where she was a talented seamstress. His sons Marvin and Anthony relocated to Planter around 1919. Pictured here from left to right are Ernest, Hilda, Anthony, and Robert.

This picture, taken in September 1967, shows an aging Ernest, Anna, Marvin, and Anthony, still wearing his pith helmet. Because their father had made a great deal of money with his Thompson Cigar Company, his children were afforded the relative comfort of knowing they could get financial help from him should they need it. Tony led more of a bohemian lifestyle as a poet, while Marvin was more driven. He helped to develop Planter's Palma Sola neighborhood as well as the road Tree Lane. Marvin was also elected justice of the peace. He was something of a writer himself, penning the foreword to Nikki Beare's 1961 Florida Keys guidebook, *Pirates, Pineapples, and People*, as well as a book of his own in 1971, *Florida Real Estate: An Introduction to the Profession*.

Marvin Thompson's younger brother Tony was a poet who had several poems published in anthologies. He also had a penchant for raising tomatoes. Locals boasted that they were the best in all of the Keys. Tony made a habit of staying in any open house left unattended and helping himself to whatever was in the kitchen. This photograph was taken in 1982.

Marvin Thompson is wearing his pith helmet in this photograph. The man hammering away at what will become a cistern house is Jack Wilkinson, no relation to author Jerry Wilkinson. The picture was taken January 28, 1936.

By the 1930s, Planter was practically a ghost town. Besides the Thompson brothers, the only other person calling Planter home was Jack Wilkinson. The MIT-educated Pan Am aircraft mechanic was unhappy with his job in Miami. He quit in 1936 and moved to Key Largo. This photograph, taken in August 1936, shows Jack standing beside the finished cistern house.

When Jack arrived in Planter, he never bought land but was more of a squatter who drove out to the end of Planter Street and pitched a tent. To make money, he collected live fish (and mammals) for Marine Studios. He was drafted by the armed forces in 1942. This picture was taken in 1937.

Jack Wilkinson met his wife, Katharine Mata, in the Miami suburb of Coral Gables. Katharine was called "Kay." The two married in Fort Lauderdale, and Jack brought her to his Planter home. This photograph, shot about 1939, shows the Wilkinsons throwing a party. Jack is seated at far left, and Kay is holding up a bottle. Kay captioned this photograph: "Life in the Keys has not changed."

The goal of Marine Studios when it opened in June 1938 was to provide a realistic underwater stage for filming scenes for motion pictures and newsreels. The facility would later become St. Augustine's Marineland. Jack Wilkinson collected marine specimens from Key Largo waters. The base for his operation was Planter. Note the large transportation tank on the back of the truck. Saylor Watson, Jack's best friend, is pictured here.

In the 1950s, Joe Burton decided to have the old waterfront of Planter dredged to create a marina at the end of Planter Street, at one time the site of the old Planter Pier and home to the Wilkinsons. Docks were constructed, and the site was landscaped with royal palm trees. The end result was the Burton Yacht Harbor. This photograph was taken around 1951.

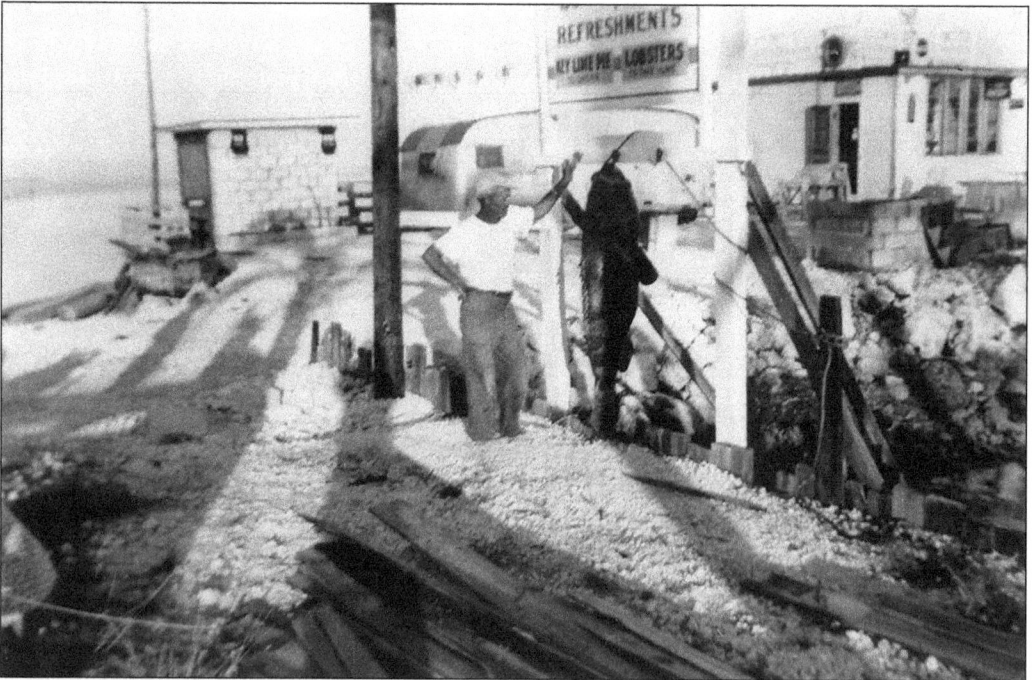

In addition to the yacht basin, a small restaurant and store was established at the water's edge and operated by Marvin Thompson. Key lime pie was made to order, and fresh spiny lobsters were available. It is unclear who the man in the picture is, but the fish hanging on the hook is a jewfish, called today a goliath grouper. Hurricane Donna destroyed the small marina in 1960.

This March 16, 1958, aerial photograph shows a rather undeveloped Planter community. The main arteries have been carved out of the hammock. Burton Drive enters from US highway 1 at left. Where Burton Drive, named after Joe Burton, elbows in the direction of the Atlantic is Planter Street, where the Planter Pier, Jack Wilkinson, and the Burton Yacht Harbor once existed. HHP stands for Harry Harris Park.

This house, built in 1958, belonged to Earl Krebs. The picture was taken from an airplane or helicopter surveying damage from Hurricane Donna. The tidal surge from Donna was over seven feet, and the seaweed left behind was up to the first-floor doorknob. Kreb rebuilt after the storm. The image shows how undeveloped Harry Harris Park was in 1960. It is now home to author and historian Jerry Wilkinson.

This image shows what a hurricane as strong as Donna is capable of. As the storm approached Key Largo, its energy was sufficient to suck the waters of Florida Bay away from the island. The photograph was taken by the house caretaker of Dr. Fred Bond, who lived in a home on Florida Bay near mile marker 94.

This photograph was also taken by the caretaker of Dr. Bond's house and shows what happened when the other side of Donna struck the island. When the wind changed direction, the waters of Florida Bay were pushed back toward shore. The category 4 hurricane pushed a tidal surge of nine feet onto the island.

Harris Park   Florida Keys

This postcard of the Planter area is from about 1960. The beach in the center of the image is the county park, Harry Harris Park. Though technically still considered Planter, the community has since become known as simply Harry Harris. While the street system is fully developed here, the roads have yet to be lined with the rows of houses that fill the neighborhood today.

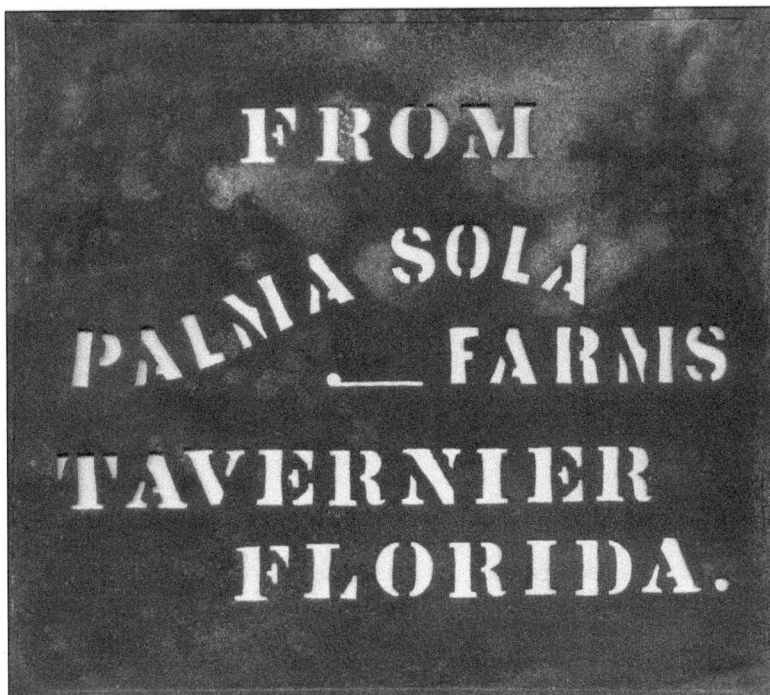

FROM
PALMA SOLA
FARMS
TAVERNIER
FLORIDA.

This brass stencil comes from the extensive historical collection of Jerry Wilkinson. It was used to mark packing crates filled with produce harvested from the Palma Sola Farms. Palma Sola is a subdivision of the Planter community developed by C. Marvin Thompson. The stencil identifies the farm's location as Tavernier.

An early resident of the second incarnation of the Planter community was a man known as John "the Dutchman" Rickter. According to one of Marvin Thompson's nieces, Rickter liked to be barefoot and would sometimes help her uncle at his Burton Yacht Harbor store. This is a photograph of John the Dutchman's house taken by the Monroe County property adjuster in 1960.

By the time this photograph was taken in 1982, there was not much left of the old Planter Pier. The photographer stands on what remains of the pier and is looking south over what would have been the original community of Planter. Once upon a time, this was where the Samuel Johnson family homes stood. Today, it is home to the Ocean Pointe Condominium complex.

Seven

ROCK HARBOR

For the Florida East Coast Railway, the Jewfish Creek Bridge was the gateway to Key Largo and the Florida Keys. This undated photograph of the Jewfish Station shows the train's first stop on the island. Jewfish Station, as well as those communities on the island of Key Largo north of Tavernier, would become known as Rock Harbor.

On November 15, 1921, Lillian Sexton was appointed postmaster of the Key Largo Post Office. Sexton moved to Key Largo from Missouri with her husband, Charles. Their dream was to create a "Venice in the Keys," to which end Charles blasted and dredged a series of canals referred to these days as Sexton Cove. This undated photograph shows one of the Sexton buildings near mile marker 105. It once housed the post office, as the sign just above the head of the man at left indicates. The building also operated as the Key Largo Store, according to the sign nailed into the tree trunk at right. In addition to the post office and general store, the Sextons ran a hotel. In 1926, the *Key Largo Breeze* advertised Charlie Sexton's land clearing and dredging services. The Key Largo Post Office closed March 15, 1936, and the mail was rerouted to the first Rock Harbor Post Office, which used to be near mile marker 100.

Scheduled train service had been established between Miami and Marathon by January 1908. The island of Key Largo had four scheduled stops: Jewfish, Key Largo, Rock Harbor, and Tavernier. The Key Largo Depot is shown in this c. 1920 photograph. The telegraph station was located here at the Key Largo Depot. The building was near mile marker 105.6, just south of where the Key Largo Chamber of Commerce stands today.

By the 1920s, the Upper Keys were shipping as many as 60,000 crates of key limes annually. One of the larger producers of limes in the area was H.M. Hull, who owned seven groves. C.C. Chapman managed the groves. Hull had his own packing plant, once located near Key Largo Depot at mile marker 105.5. This photograph shows what was left of the packing plant after a 1926 hurricane.

Key Largo's Stillwright Point, located in Blackwater Sound, is a corruption of the German name Stellrecht, meaning cartwright. The name comes from the Stellrecht family. Emil Otto Stellrecht, born in 1904 to Otto Stellrecht and Isabelle Ann Pinder, is shown in this undated image with his fingers inside the gills of a big snook. Note the barbed gigging pole balanced atop the boat.

Charles B. MacPherson operated Rock Harbor's Mac's Place with his wife, Ann. Mac's used to be found at mile marker 98.2. There is a description of it in the 1938 book *U.S. one, Maine to Florida*, which reads: "Mac's Place where cabins, sea foods, gasoline and boats are available. Sportsmen starting out to catch bonefish often buy supplies here." The postcard is postmarked 1934.

This is a 1910 portrait of George L. Engel. He was a New Jersey dentist who moved to Key Largo with his wife, Anna, in the 1920s. A March 29, 1938, article about the Oversea Highway, printed in Ohio's *Mansfield News Journal*, stated that Engel had been in poor health when he began gathering coral rock for the foundation of a family home. Though his health reportedly improved, Dr. Engel died in 1945.

Dr. Engel managed to build something a little more than a mere island home, as this c. 1940 photograph shows. It is still referred to as the Largo Sound Rock Castle. Built to resemble a European castle, the walls are three feet thick at the base and taper to 16 inches at the top. The castle is one of the oldest structures in the Upper Keys still standing in its original location.

This photograph of the Engel castle was taken about 1940 and shows the home's elaborate towers. After the Great Labor Day Hurricane of 1935, the Engel property became known as the Haunted House on Largo Sound. The tidal surge resulting from the storm pushed water over the island. The ground floor of the Engel home became flooded, and while Anna Engel weathered the storm safely inside one of the home's towers, the terrified woman listened in horror as the Atlantic Ocean washed over the island and pooled inside her home. As water filled the first floor of the building, the furniture began to rise and as it did, the tidal surge swirled inside the home, knocking the chairs and tables against the castle's walls over and over again. The event reportedly traumatized Anna Engel. When the storm waters receded, the phantom knocking was said to have continued.

Published in 1938, *U.S. one, Maine to Florida*, written by the Federal Writer's Project working within the Works Progress Administration, described Rock Harbor as "a tiny village with a 30-foot Observation Tower over its post office. The tower is a square stucco structure anchored by cables to the bedrock; from its railed upper platform is a view of the Atlantic, Florida Bay, and the Gulf. Eastward is the ocean shore, where there are racks for fish nets. All around the tiny settlement are extensive lime groves that bear most of the year; to the W. is a mango grove." The building, owned by C.O. Garret, operated as a post office and appears to have been a general store of sorts as well. "See The Beautiful Keys From This Tower No Charge" is painted on the front of the building beneath the Rock Harbor Post Office sign.

This photograph was taken around 1940. The Curry family is standing in front of the family enterprise. Pictured from left to right are John and Elizabeth Curry, Floyd, Cyril and Bertha Curry, and John and Cyril's father, Norman Curry. Norman emigrated to the Keys from the Bahamas. At left is a Standard Oil station and next to it is an early Rock Harbor Post Office. Two chairs can be seen to either side of the open door. This enclave was once found at approximately mile marker 100. The post office was later moved about a half mile to the south, near what is today the Napa auto parts store. The family is standing in front of John and Elizabeth's home. John's Rock Harbor School bus is parked beside his home.

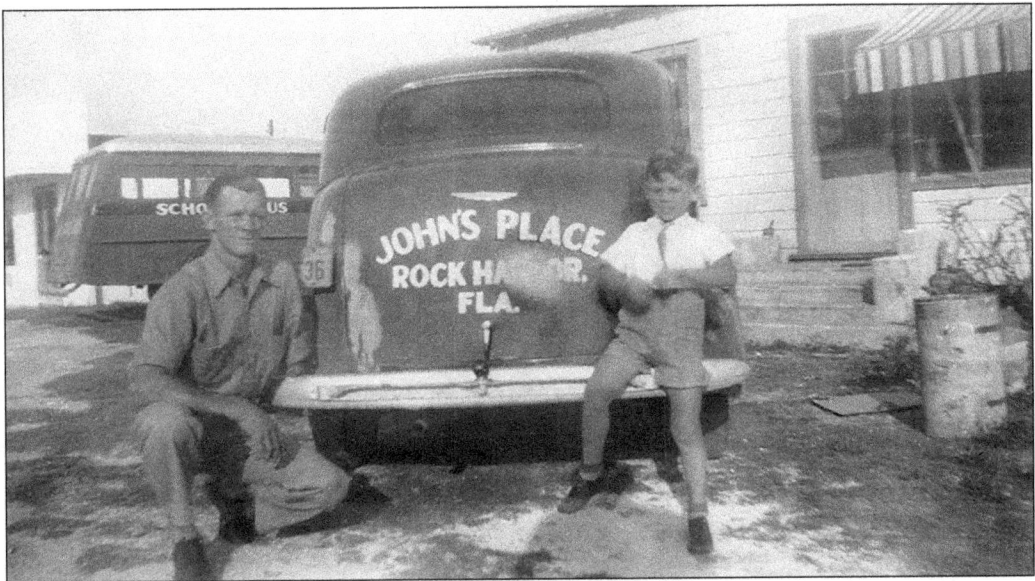

Norman Curry moved to Key West from Green Turtle Cay, Bahamas. He would later move to Rock Harbor and marry Ellen Bethel. Their son John, pictured in this undated photograph, was the Rock Harbor School bus driver. Remarkably, all the shifting and steering required to navigate the rough road was done by a man with one arm.

The date of this photograph is unknown, but the bus driver, standing near the driver's side door of the school bus, is John Curry. The Rock Harbor Grammar School used to be located in what is now the median of the highway at approximately mile marker 98.5. The building is still standing, in a manner. It is now the Moose Lodge.

When the Caribbean Club was first developed it was a private fishing club, constructed by Carl Fisher, a Miami Beach developer. Poor health precluded Carl from attending the January 1940 grand opening. Tom Hanley was hired to operate the club. He purchased the property in 1945 and added the six-room hotel wing. Allegedly, a not-too-secret gambling casino was in operation there during the tourist season.

This image is identified as a Steinmartz photograph and was shot in the early 1950s. It shows the interior of the Caribbean Club's dining room. Photographs on display on the wall include portraits of John Huston, Lauren Bacall, and Humphrey Bogart, the stars of the movie that put the Caribbean Club on the map.

The Humphrey Bogart and Lauren Bacall classic *Key Largo* was not filmed at the Caribbean Club. However, the film was born here. Director John Huston and screenwriter Richard Brooks stayed at the hotel while writing the screen adaptation of the 1939 play written by Maxwell Anderson. Huston liked the title of the Maxwell Anderson play, but did not like the content. Brooks reworked the script beneath the coconut palms shading the grounds of the fishing club. It is reported that Huston and Brooks did a little gambling during their stay at the club, with Huston losing as much as $25,000 to Hanley's craps tables and roulette wheel. Brooks lost a reported $6,000, about the pay for his script. Legend suggests that while a hurricane was bearing down on the island the day the two were set to leave, the director and writer managed to gamble their debts down to only a few thousand each.

This undated photograph shows the dedication of the new Caribbean Club road sign. In 1955, a fire destroyed the six-room hotel addition Tom Hanley attached to the club. The scandal of the day, however, was that a Miami woman supposedly died in the room of a Long Island doctor. A criminal investigation ensued. Ruth Whitehurst bought the property from Richard Craig in 1962.

After the notoriety John Huston's *Key Largo* brought to the island, the residents of the community of Rock Harbor passed around a petition to have the town's name changed to Key Largo. The Rock Harbor Post Office ceased to exist on May 31, 1952, and the Key Largo Post Office opened on June 1. The outline of the original building near the Curry house is still visible.

Harry Sonntag was born October 12, 1900, in Astoria, New York, and studied painting at the Pratt Institute of Art. His Manhattan gallery, as well as his work, was destroyed by fire in the 1940s. Harry took off hitchhiking and spent years travelling through California, Washington, and Wisconsin before hitching south to the Florida Keys. He settled on Key Largo, north of what is today the Mandalay Marina.

Sonntag found his way to Rock Harbor and built a shack out of driftwood and tarpaper in the 1940s. He kept a fire burning and bathed his exposed flesh in smoke to keep the biting bugs away. He built his home close to a small bay where he fished and washed himself. He kept a small garden of greens and tomatoes. For the first two years, this was his home and studio.

113

On Sunday, July 6, 1952, a story titled "Harry J. Sonntag Lives for Art Alone," ran in the *Miami Daily News*. "Art," Harry Sonntag was quoted as saying, "is the universal language, and my desire is to bring beauty to the multitudes, so that people may realize how lovely the world is." To that end, the brilliant displays of sunrise and sunset colors became his palette, and nature became his inspiration.

Harry Sonntag, "the Hermit Artist of Key Largo," opened his Key Largo Art Gallery in 1951. The gallery was an abandoned key lime packinghouse. The rent was perfect for Harry—free! He painted only two signs to advertise his gallery, an "Open" sign for the door and the sign on the roof. The gallery was located near mile marker 97.5. Despite the sign, it was often closed.

A Harry Sonntag painting was not cheap. Prices ranged between $55 and $65, or about $500 to $600 in today's money. Harry's prices were non-negotiable, and patrons making lower offers were ignored even when he could use the money. The one thing that was clear about Harry Sonntag was that he had no interest in becoming rich.

Jack Reilly was a fishing guide captain who charted the cruiser *Swabbie*. He also operated the Gulfstream Fishing Lodge, pictured in this postcard postmarked November 1950. The fishing resort was capable of servicing as many as 28 guests. The first four buildings appear to be accommodations; the last building functioned as the cocktail lounge. The lodge was destroyed by fire on April 15, 1958, with losses estimated at $90,000.

The Land-Ho! was once found at mile marker 94.7, near where the Dove Creek Lodge Building is today. This c. 1952 postcard shows the roadside restaurant featuring outside seating with umbrellas set up along the Oversea Highway. As well as offering an assortment of more typical Keys cuisine, the Land-Ho! declared itself famous for its banana bread.

This image from the first annual Key Lime Festival in 1953 features, from left to right, Joanne Byrum, Key Largo princess; Carolyn Smith, Islamorada princess; Barbara "Babs" Kaufman, Islamorada princess; Dorothy Albury, Islamorada queen; and Jackie Sweeting, Islamorada princess. According to newspaper accounts, several thousand people attended, dined at a fish fry, and watched a parade of decorated yachts.

On April 28, 1955, the *Florida Keys News* reported: "A petition is being circulated in Key Largo, relevant to relocating the site of the new Negro School to be built in that area. The petition asks for a change of the location from the site originally selected. It is pointed out that property values are too high in this spot to be used for this purpose and to relocate the school on property of less commercial value." The Burlington Grammar School was a one-room house moved from Tavernier. The building held classes for grades one through nine; it was relocated to mile marker 101, Oceanside, near where the Key Largo Mosquito Control Building is today. The school closed in February 1965 when Monroe County integrated its school system and relocated students to Coral Shores School on Plantation Key. This photograph, taken in 1969, shows the building housing the Allen African Methodist Episcopal Church.

The machine in this photograph was used to excavate the Key Largo Waterway. It was invented, built, and patented by Bernard "Barney" Waldin. It was able to cut deep trenches through coral rock and consisted of two D-8 Caterpillar engines mounted, at right angles, one on top of the other. The lower engine moved the machine forward while the top engine rotated a track constructed with steel cutting blades that churned through the coral rock. Marvin Dow Adams, an insurance man from Miami who moved to the Keys and developed the Anglers Park subdivision, conceived the Key Largo Waterway. The canal, the only throughway between Angelfish Creek and Tavernier Creek, took a year and a half to excavate. The walls of the half-mile-long canal are 15 feet tall and have an average water depth of 25 feet. Named Adams Cut, the passage opened to boat traffic on February 26, 1961. It is now called the Marvin Adams Waterway.

John D. Pennekamp was born January 1, 1897, in Cincinnati, Ohio. He was likely born a newspaperman and started in the business as a copy boy at 14. At 28, he moved to the edge of Florida's swampland to cover the Miami land bust. He wrote for the *Miami Herald* for 50 years. Pennekamp fell in love with the South Florida land and water and was at least partly responsible for a large part of Florida swampland being declared Everglades National Park. It was Pennekamp who proposed a park to help protect at least a sampling of the coral reefs along the third largest barrier reef system in the world. "The situation has become desperate," said Pennekamp. "The souvenir purveyors are out there with barges taking it apart." Dynamite was used to break the reef into small enough pieces to satisfy the souvenir trade. The proposed Coral Reef Preserve was the first effort to protect the Florida Reef. The park encompasses approximately 70 square nautical miles of mangroves, seagrass, and coral reefs.

The Coral Reef Reserve set a record for the fastest park to germinate from proposal to opening day. Dr. Gilbert Voss of the Marine Institute noted, "Seldom has an idea gained such momentum with so little resistance." This photograph was taken at Harry Harris Park on December 10, 1960, where, to honor the newspaperman who championed the idea, Gov. Leroy Collins dedicated John D. Pennekamp Coral Reef State Park.

This c. 1961 photograph shows, from left to right, Johnny Johnson, John Pennekamp, Ellison Hardee, and Joe Fredricks standing on the beach at the park. Ellison Hardee was the park's first superintendent. Today, the world's first underwater park attracts about one million visitors every year and has become synonymous with snorkeling over the coral reef.

This statue is found at St. Justin the Martyr Catholic Church at mile marker 105.5. It is a replica of *Christ of the Deep*, created by Italian sculptor Professor Guido Galletti in 1954 to inspire all those who explored and loved the sea. The third casting of the nine-foot-tall statue, commissioned by Italian dive equipment–manufacturer Egidio Cressi, was donated to the Underwater Society of America in 1961.

The statue was packed inside a wooden crate and shipped aboard the SS *Extravia*. It arrived at New York Harbor's Navy Pier in 1963. Carl M. Hueber, president of the Underwater Society of America, accepted the statue, and it was temporarily stored at Chicago's O'Hare Airport. Florida senator Spessard Holland lobbied to have the prize awarded to John D. Pennekamp Coral Reef State Park.

The statue began its journey to Florida in January 1964. The package arrived at Pennekamp in the spring of 1965. Before it was transported out to the reef, the statue was fitted atop an 11-foot tiered concrete support base, poured by the park's staff. Combined, the statue and the base weighed approximately 20,000 pounds. In this photograph, park superintendent Ellison Hardee is pictured in the foreground.

On August 25, 1965, the *Christ of the Deep* settled comfortably beneath the Atlantic surface, 25 feet down, at the reef site Key Largo Dry Rocks. Two weeks later, Hurricane Betsy blew across the Upper Keys. The statue stood tall and was unaffected by the storm and was officially dedicated by John Pennekamp on June 29, 1966. Today, it is the single most photographed object on the Florida Reef.

The Monroe County property appraiser took this photograph of Mac and Marie MacQuarrie's restaurant in February 1965. Mac and Marie's restaurant was considered one of the best on the island and was famous for glazed "Old time roaster corn on the cob" and for serving "Fine food a little different." One of the sandwich boards out front advertises both Gourmet and Gourmand food like spicy fried yellowtail snapper, conch, and turtle steaks, but there was no bar.

One of the first students to attend the Burlington Grammar School was Harry Davis Jr. The Davis family, Harry Sr. and Florence, his wife, moved to the Keys from Andros, Bahamas, and can be documented in the Newport area from the early 1900s. Harry Davis Jr. became a volunteer fireman in 1958 and chief of the Key Largo Volunteer Fire Department in 1971. He retired in 1975.

The name "Wee" Wynken Blyken and Nod Estates stems from a Dutch lullaby written by Eugene Field on March 9, 1889. Found on the Atlantic side near mile marker 96, this 1971 image shows a trailer park. The village is now a collection of both mobile and upscale homes and might be best known for its curious collection of road names including Thumper Thoroughfare, Humpty Dumpty Drive, and Little Miss Muffett Lane.

Trailer park communities were once prevalent in the Florida Keys. Many have been replaced by resort properties and waterfront homes. This modern aerial photograph shows Captain Jax's Trailer Park, considered an RV resort. The property is located next to the U-Haul storage facility near mile marker 103.6. The photograph also gives a clear view of the Marvin Adams Cut to the right of the storage facility.

The *Livingstone* was commissioned by the British East African Railroad in 1912 and shipped to the Congo. John Huston and Sam Spiegel bought the boat in 1950 for use in the 1951 production *African Queen*, starring Humphrey Bogart and Katharine Hepburn. Jim Hendricks Sr., one-time owner of the Key Largo Holiday Inn, acquired the 28-foot steam engine–propelled *African Queen* in 1982 for $65,000. Jim Hendricks Sr. died in 2002.

The *African Queen* became a Key Largo tourist attraction in the 1980s. Jim Hendricks Jr., who operates the gift shop at Key Largo's Holiday Inn at mile marker 100, leased the storied vessel to Lance and Suzanne Holmquist in 2011. They have completely refurbished the *African Queen*, and it is once again taking passengers on scenic tours through the mangrove channels and bays of Key Largo's picturesque waters.

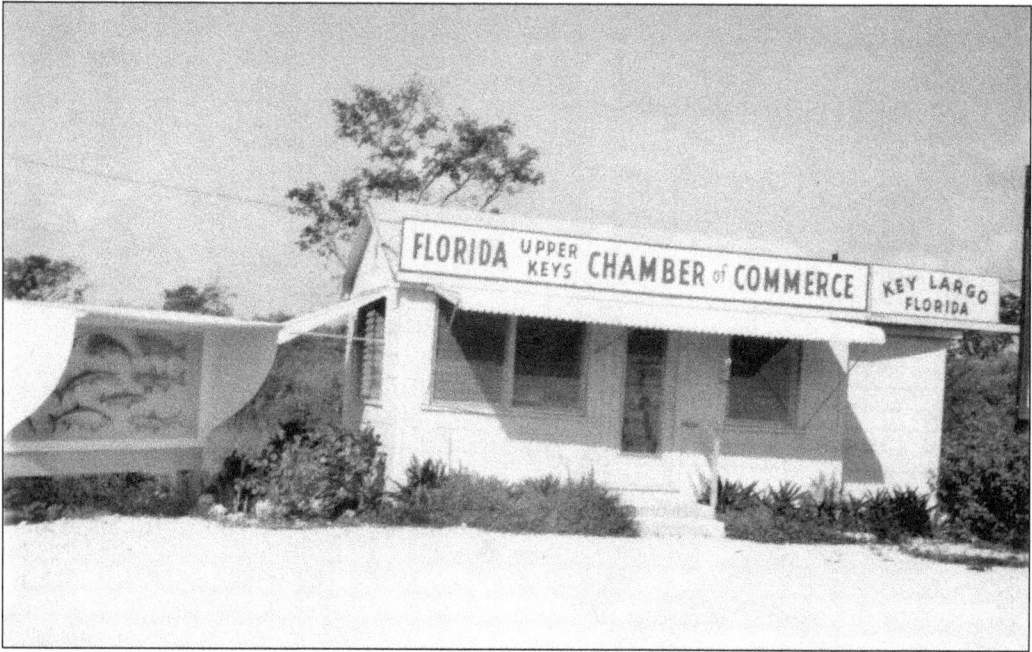

The *Florida Keys Weekly News* announced, "The Upper Keys Chamber of Commerce was officially organized Thursday, May 29, 1947. Officers for the year were elected as follows: president, Mr. Mckenzie; vice president, Alonzo Cothron; secretary, F.A. Calhoun; and treasurer, Mr. McRae. The first thing on their program is starting a summer Fishing Tournament for the Upper Keys."

This c. 1960 postcard shows the old Jewfish Creek Bridge that was first built in 1943. The house at the base of the bridge was the home of the bridge tender, first for the Florida East Coast Railway and then the Oversea Highway. The double-bascule drawbridge was torn down after the new bridge opened to traffic in 2008.

William Beauregard Albury was born on Key West in 1886. His family moved to Key Largo weeks later. In 1913, William helped his father, William Dunham, build this Bahamian-style house and would continue to live in it for 42 years. The building is the oldest structure in Key Largo still standing in its original locale. Found at mile marker 98.3, it is now home to the Reef Environmental Education Foundation.

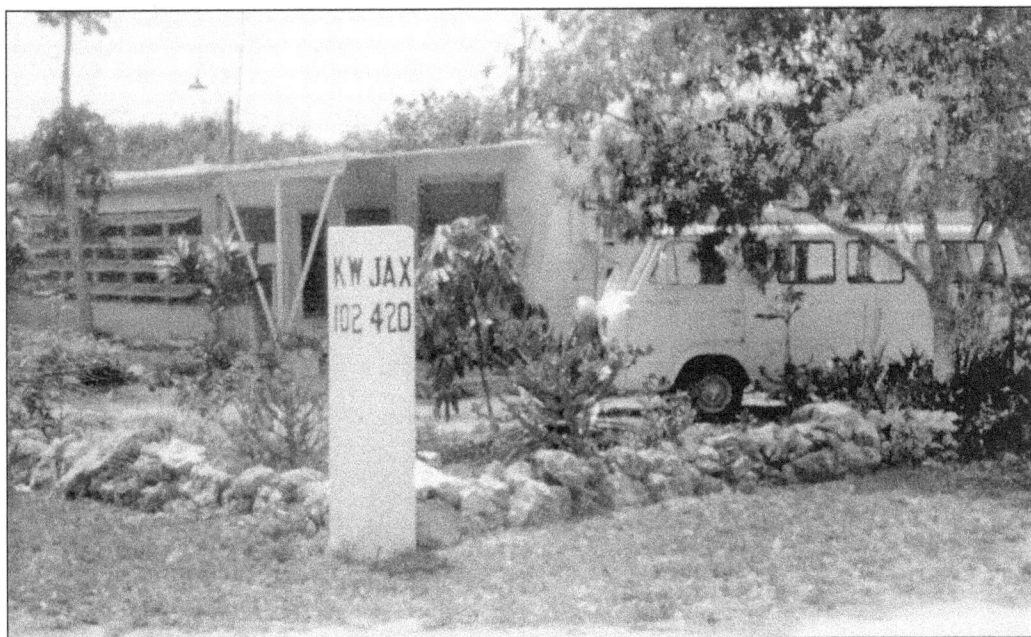

Mile markers have been posted along the Florida Keys since the railroad days. Two sets of numbers were displayed on the old markers, the number of miles to Key West and to Jacksonville. This photograph, taken March 26, 1971, shows one of the two original mile markers still standing. It has been relocated behind the Caribbean Club. The other marker is located at the Lower Keys Chamber of Commerce on Big Pine Key.

Visit us at
arcadiapublishing.com

www.ingramcontent.com/pod-product-compliance
Lightning Source LLC
Chambersburg PA
CBHW050642110426
42813CB00007B/1893